Quarndon:
Then & Now

Editor
Bryan Harris

Published by
Quarndon Parish Council

© Bryan Harris, 2008

First published in Great Britain in 2008
by Quarndon Parish Council

Copyright © 2008 Bryan Harris

All rights reserved.
No part of this publication may be reproduced, stored
in a retrieval system, or transmitted in any form or by
any means - electronic, mechanical, photocopying,
recording or otherwise - without the prior permission
of both the copyright owner and the above publisher of
the book.

A CIP catalogue record of this book is available from
the British Library.

ISBN 978-0-9559158-0-2

Typeset in Gill Sans by Copper Dog Limited, Derbyshire.
Printed and bound by Print Partners International Ltd.

Supported by The National Lottery
through the Heritage Lottery Fund.

Printed on natural, renewable and recyclable paper
sourced from wood grown in sustainable forests.

www.quarndon.parishcouncil.net

then&now@quarndon.parishcouncil.net

Contents

Foreword

By the Rev'd WILLIAM BATES, Priest-in-Charge, St Paul's, Quarndon

I was glad to be asked to write a *Foreword* to *Quarndon: Then & Now* - not least because it allows me to pay tribute to a community-minded man who has gone to great lengths to piece together a history of his adopted village.

There are a number of ways in which history can be written, but Bryan Harris describes his book as a 'chronicle of record'. He has taken a largely matter of fact approach to both past and present and, ordering his material into 35 chapters, has combined historical records, expert contributions and personal memories. He has collaborated with others and, in particular, has provided an excellent pictorial account of village features and personalities. On behalf of all who have the interests of Quarndon at heart, it gives me great pleasure to thank him.

In the broader context of the history of Derbyshire, Quarndon is virtually a footnote. For centuries it was an ecclesiastical satellite of what is now Derby Cathedral. Later it became a spa village that never quite fulfilled the ambitions of its proponents. As its agricultural life declined, Quarndon began to change into a suburban village for managers and entrepreneurs in the industries of Derby. Probably the most momentous event in its history was the relatively late Enclosure Act of 1816 by which an elite community destroyed a longstanding way of rural living and paved the way for the then almost sacrilegious notion that common land might become a desirable residential postcode.

However, the importance of Quarndon on a county level is beside the point, for there is much of interest in any inhabited area. As Bryan Harris draws this out in ways that allow the evidence to speak for itself, the question that he has posed for me centres on what it means to be a community. Chapter 32 shows how various attempts have been made to organise special events - ideally for all residents. The participation of a good number of people has been regarded as a demonstration of successful community life. On the other hand, Chapters 13, 23 and 25, among others, suggest that community lies in a variety of semi-independent, but often over-lapping, interest groups. What matters are the relationships which people form with each other and their readiness to be 'good neighbours'.

Another concept of community is to view it as consisting of symbols to which people attach a range of meanings. Thus St Paul's Church, the Curzon School and *The Joiners' Arms* are highly visible symbols of Quarndon, but the meanings which villagers attach to them are in some senses shared and in others different. As symbols like the village shop are lost, people's sense of belonging to Quarndon is likely, in general terms, to decline unless new symbols are added. Of course not all symbols of community take the form of buildings and Bryan's book shows how community life is continually being restated. At a time when many view the village as a place for private residence, what forms will active participants be able to give to community life in the future?

These comments go beyond the scope of *Quarndon: Then & Now*, the aim of which is, essentially, to inform. However, as the book stimulates interest in the village, it has the potential to become, in itself, a symbol of community. My hope for the book is that, as it has sprung out of a love for Quarndon, it will create conversation and action that reflect a similar love. And that, as the book travels further afield, it will awaken interest in local and regional history.

To Liz, Jonathan & Charlotte;

for their love & forbearance!

Introduction: How this book came about

By BRYAN HARRIS

QUARNDON:*Then & Now* has experienced a gestation period longer than that of any known mammal! Its conception took place in 1986, soon after I became a member of Quarndon Parish Council.

Under an agenda item called "Parish Chest" it was proposed that, before being deposited in the County Record Office at Matlock, the Council's documents - dating back to 1894 - should be put on display for the benefit of Quarndon residents. When I asked what the documents consisted of I was told that they included *Land Tax Assessments, Rate Books, Overseers' Reports, Quarndon's Enclosure Award,* etc, etc. These struck me as being mind-numbingly boring on their own, so I suggested that, in addition, we should invite villagers to raid their attics for photographs, artefacts and other memorabilia so that we could mount a fully comprehensive exhibition of Quarndon's history and way of life. This was agreed and I was duly commissioned to organise it.

I called the exhibition **Quarndon:Then & Now** and it filled the Curzon School Hall and a couple of classrooms. It took place over a long weekend and attracted a stream of visitors, including former villagers - some of whom came back several times.

Using 25 display panels, I found that the history of the village presented itself easily under 25 subject headings - *The "Old" Church, The "New" Church, The School, The Chalybeate Spring, The Joiners' Arms,* and so on. On the following pages, these panels are now converted into chapters - increased to 35, including a *Family Walk.*

Now I'm well aware that the order in which the chapters appear could be the subject of much circular argument! But suffice it to say that, as far as possible, the historical beginnings of each subject covered are set out in chronological order, with the narrative being brought up to date by the end of the chapter.

For those new to the village, at the head of most chapters the location of the area covered is indicated by a red dot - or dots - on a vignette.

Chapters without a by-line are by me, as are most of the non-attributed colour photographs and the layout of the book. Overleaf, I've expressed my appreciation of the work carried out by fellow members of the *Quarndon: Then & Now* Team. I'd also like to thank Quarndon Parish Council for agreeing to publish the book and the Heritage Lottery Fund for financing it.

So my apologies for the fact that this *magnum opus* has taken 22 years to reach the book-shelves. When I embarked on the project I was Manager of BBC Radio Derby. From 1987 to 2004 I was Chairman of Quarndon Parish Council. When I retired from the BBC in 1992 I took on the post of Communications Officer for the Diocese of Derby. In 2000/1 I chaired Quarndon's Millennium Committee, and, since 1994, I've been Chairman of the Derby Decorative & Fine Arts Society. The result has been that, all too often, *Quarndon: Then & Now* became relegated to the role of **"Quarndon: Now & Then"**!

However, better late than never, I hope this 'chronicle of record' will stimulate your interest in the life and history of this medium-sized Derbyshire village, set in the local, national - and sometimes international - context of the Second Millennium.   >>>

My thanks are due to my nine colleagues of the *Quarndon: Then & Now* **Editorial Team:**

Don Hall, for his research and photography.

Rosemary Lucas, for her advice on local and industrial history.

Ann Ousley, for transcribing all the local interviews and for final proof-reading.

Matthew Pitt, for maps and explanations regarding boundaries, turnpikes and enclosures.

James Richardson, for his local reminiscences and detailed attention to the text.

Noel Tornbohm, for his historical research and maps.

Clare Turner, for trawling through the text and compiling the *Family Walk*.

David Widdows, for his extensive photography throughout the book.

My wife, **Liz**, for her roles as business manager, in helping to secure the Heritage Lottery Fund Grant and as a final proof-reader.

Acknowledgements

The Editor has appreciated the recorded reminiscences of the following:

 Frank Stone, Clerk to Quarndon Parish Council from 1963 to 1977, former Captain, Quarndon Cricket Club, and a key source of information for *Quarndon: Then & Now*

 The late **Ivan Cope**, who moved to Quarndon as a child in 1926

 Harold Coulthread, who farmed in Quarndon for 46 years

 The late **Ursula Eddowes**, former Chairman of Quarndon Parish Council, who spent her childhood and 'teens at Park Nook

 The late **Arthur Heathcote, Jnr**, son of **Arthur Heathcote**, village blacksmith & postman

 The late **Mary Jepson**, daughter of **Bill Beeby**, the village coachman, carrier and coalman

 The late **Fred Kelsey**, who spent his childhood at *Bottom Farm*

 Maria Maier, of *Beech Cottages*, widow of a former German prisoner of war

 Maurice Oakley, who spent his childhood at *Burley Grange Farm*

The finished book is the result of research carried out at the Derby Local Studies Library, Derby Museums & Art Gallery, the County Record Office, Matlock, the Muniment Room at *Kedleston Hall* and through the Head Teachers' Logs and Managers' Minutes from the Curzon School.

There has been considerable reliance on three articles in **Derbyshire Life & Countryside** - one by Frank Constable, former Parks Superintendent, Derby City Council, and two by the local historian, the late **Roy Christian**.

The following books and theses have also featured in my researches:

The late **Ellen Hampshire's Quarndon**, written for the Quarndon Women's Institute in 1931.

Historical Vignettes of Quarndon by the late **Margery Sulley & Reginald Wibberley** (Published by Quarndon Women's Institute)

Derek A Wigley's Quarndon: An Illustrated History

H Hall & A L Sulley: Quarndon Parish Church & the Curzon Church of England School

Noel Tornbohm's Leicester University English Local History MA thesis: Facets of Enclosure in a Mid-Derbyshire Manor (1760-1860)

Rosemary Lucas: Quarndon Old Hall & 17th Century Village

Joan D'Arcy: A City within a City: Little Chester, Derby, AD80-AD2000

Linda Owen's Nottingham University Advanced Certificate in Local History thesis: Quarndon: Parish & Village

Roy Christian: Derbyshire (Batsford, 1978)

Bulmer's History, Topography & Directory: Derbyshire

Llewellyn Jewitt: The Ceramic Art of Great Britain (Virtue & Co)

Kenneth Cameron: English Place Names (Batsford, 1996)

Other acknowledgements are due to the following. (NB: I have not distinguished between those still alive and those who have since died.)

Ian Aitken, Philip & Sheila Aldridge, Clifford Aldwinckle, June Allen, Martin Allen, Mike & Sue Allen, Lesley Anderson, Thelma Ashton, Jonathan & Sheila Balmer, John & Shirley Banham, Jill Banks (archivist), Peter & Sylvia Bateman, the Rev'd William Bates, Belper North Mill Trust, Nancy Bird, Pam Bottomley, Simon & Rose Bousfield, Geoff & Hazel Brecknell, Canon Andy Brown, Iain Campbell, Bob Carey (Derby Diocesan Secretary), Bob Cashmore, Tom Cashmore, Ellen Cholerton, James Cholerton, Colin & Jane Clarke (volunteer researchers), Barbara Clough, Tony Clifford, John & Mary Coe, Mary Connell, Graham Cook, Betty Cope, Pamela Copestake (illustrator), Max Craven, Michael Crawley, Jocelyne Cunningham, John Cunningham (final proof-reader), the Hon. Richard Curzon, the Curzon School (Geraldine Lowdham, Head Teacher, and children of the School; Brian Windscheffel & Paul Clayton, former Head Teachers; Anne Devonport, former Deputy Head Teacher; Janice Kiernan, former Infants' teacher; Mary Wilson, School Secretary, and Heather Whitworth, née Smith, former pupil).

Joan D'Arcy, Derby Museums & Art Gallery (Anneke Bambery, Jonathan Wallis), David Dykes, Elaine Ellis, Donald & Muriel Entwisle, Mike & Lesley Etwell, Mike Evans (Chairman-Emeritus, Rolls-Royce Heritage Trust), former evacuees to Quarndon (John Doman, Edna Blake-Dawson, Roland Darvill, Bob & Peter Allen, Muriel Hardy, Audrey Bowers).

John & Freda Fallon, David & Lucy Farish, John Farnsworth, Pat Farrington, John Fasal, Margaret Fearn, Margaret Foreman, Ronald Fitzgerald, Chris Frith (illustrator), Jack & Beryl Frost, Peter Gadsby, Roy & Fiona Galloway, Doris Geeson, Ralph Gell, Bert German, Tony Glover, Ruth Good, Jacqueline Goodall.

Melanie Hall, Philip Hall (Sir Henry Royce Memorial Foundation), Robert Hamilton, Joan Handley, our son, Jonathan Harris (for suggesting the vignettes and for my prolonged use of his former bedroom as the "Book" Room), Arthur Heathcote, Ernest Heathcote, Kevin Heathcote, Michael Heathcote, Bernard Hempell (@ Web Developments) for his assistance with desktop publishing, Katherine Hines, Dr Paul Hodson, Pat Hollands, Carolyn Holton (Clerk to Quarndon Parish Council), Eric Hook, Roy Hughes, Gill Hutchinson.

David Jepson, Rachel Jones, Ruth Keeling, George Kelsey, Priscilla Kidman, Tessa Kinder, Robert & Lesley Kirkland, Trevor Kitchener, James Knifton, Mike & Chris Knifton, David & Lyn Knight, Enid Knight, Richard Langley, Helen Latham, Diane Law, Yvonne Lawton, John & Kate Leather, Christine Leathley, Major Harry Loveday, Shirley Lowe, Peter Lunn.

Sylvia McCance, Roy McFarland, the Rt Hon. Patrick McLoughlin, MP, Dave McPhee, Kirstie Mackin, (formerly *Derby Evening Telegraph*), Jean Malin, Darren Marks, Edward Marshall, Trevor & Lee Martin (*Joiners' Arms*), Mary Moorcroft, the Rev'd John & Kay Morison, Joan Morley, John Morrison, our daughter, Charlotte Mullen (for her inspirational proof-reading and encouragement), our son-in-law, Paul Mullen (for his help with the design of the book cover), Dermot & Elizabeth Murray.

National Trust, *Kedleston Hall* (Victoria Flanagan, Property Manager; Archives Team: Marilyn Lindley, Ann Jones, Patricia Whatmore), C Douglas Neal, Mary Neath, Mike Norton (*Derby Evening Telegraph*), Anita Oates, Mike O'Neill, Terry Ousley, Linda Owen, Avinash Panesar (for his assistance with the *Family Walk*), Les & Pat Parkin, Peakdale Research, Professor Jonathan Powers, Don & Pauline Prime, Quarndon Cricket Club (Peter Siddall, David Ball, Steve Hollis, Chris Storr, Martin Morley), Quarndon WI.

Brenda Ray, Colin Raybould, Trevor Raybould, Jill Reed, Brian Rich (Keele University), Richardson & Linnell (auctioneers & estate agents), William & Margaret Richardson, Terry & Sue Roberts, John Robotham, the Rod Jewell Collection, John Rosser, the Rev'd David & Frances Rymer, Alan & Sue Shearer, Chris Short, Ian Smith, Graham & Kath Smith, Nick & Gretchen Smith, Hal & Jean Snooks, Tom Spiby, David Stout (Kedleston Estate), Arthur & Margery Sulley, Phil Sulley, Keith & Judith Thomas, Pat Tinkler, Jan & Janet Turnbull, Anthony Tunley.

Brenda Veitch, David Waine (former Head of Broadcasting, *BBC in the Midlands*), who introduced me to the term 'chronicle of record', John & Nadine Waldron, Vincent Ware, Canon John Warman, Gordon & Eileen Warrington, Alan West, Dorothy White, Heather Whitworth, (*Southwell Workhouse*, NT), Sylvia Widdows, Derek Wigley, Harold S Wilson, Roland & Maggie Wood, Dr Tim Woods, Sue Woore.

Deepest apologies - and thanks - to anyone who helped over the last 22 years, but whose name I may, inadvertently, have omitted, or who I may have quoted without acknowledgement.

Source unknown

Source unknown

Two aerial photographs of Quarndon
Top: c. 1946. Bottom: c. 1998

1. Quarndon: its name & location

By NOEL TORNBOHM & BRYAN HARRIS

THE village of Quarndon lies 2.8 miles NNW of Derby and 1.25 miles south of the Pennine Chain. While the word don means 'a hill or fort', the stretch of The Common from *Overfields* (No. 19) to *Quarndon Hill* (No. 76) - see red dots on the vignette *above* - would appear to be part of a *dun*, or 'hill with a flat hollow at its summit'. This may originally have been the site of a Celtic or Anglo-Saxon settlement. In Quarndon's case, the hill has undulating slopes and rises from 220 to 482 feet above sea level.

Quern

Over a thousand years, spellings of this particular Derbyshire place-name have ranged from Cornun, Querendunie, Qwerendon, Querndon, Quern, Quoordon, Quorundon, Quarendon, Corundon, Querne and Quarn to the present Quarndon - the first syllable arguably being derived from the word *cweorn*, which is Old English for quern: 'a hand-mill for grinding corn'. (The top stone, with the centre hole, is turned while the bottom stone remains stationary.)

This would - pretty decisively - produce the meaning 'Quern Hill', except that no rock has been found locally that would be hard enough for such work. However, since Quarndon is on the site of an Ice Age 'terminal moraine', it is possible that a glacier may have brought down deposits of gritstone, which, until the supply was exhausted, could have been used for hand-grinding.

Alternatively, in his book, *Quarndon: An illustrated history*, Derek A Wigley suggests that the Queren, Querne, Quarn, etc, of Quarndon is derived from the word *gwaun*, meaning 'down or moor', or that it could refer to a local tribe, whose name, the *Cornovii*, may have been misheard by some early chroniclers.

As for Quarndon's location, the original village was situated on the southern side of the hill (on either side of the current Church Road), where its inhabitants made full use of maximum sunshine, protection from northerly winds and local streams and springs - including a medicinal one, which once attracted 'spa' visitors from far and wide.

Church Road, Quarndon, today

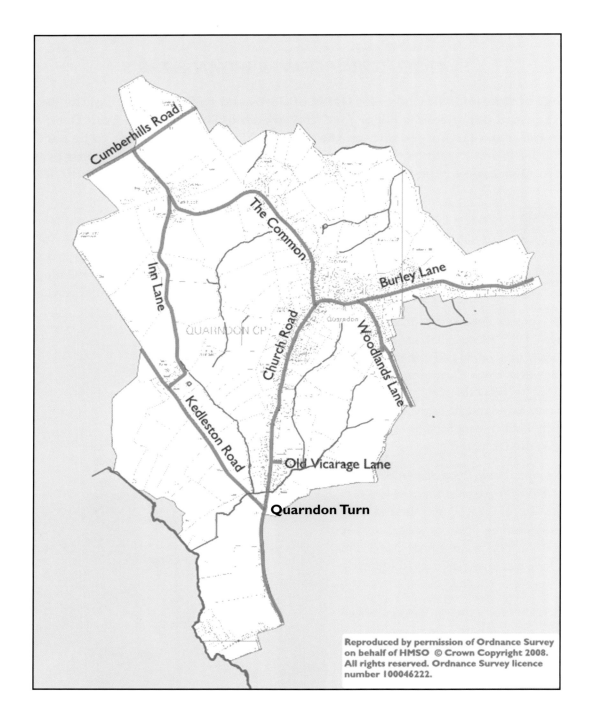

Reproduced by permission of Ordnance Survey on behalf of HMSO © Crown Copyright 2008. All rights reserved. Ordnance Survey licence number 100046222.

Quarndon's present main roads
Map by Matthew Pitt

There was certainly an early settlement around the area of the present Old Vicarage Lane, where the confluence of two streams formed a mill-pond. Until it was demolished in 1812, there was a Hall with an estate farm in the vicinity of the lane, while, to the immediate north, a Chapel with a Norman door existed until it was largely demolished in 1873-4.

Until the end of World War 2, the basic industry in the village was farming - much of the land belonging to the Curzons of *Kedleston Hall*.

Over the past three centuries, Quarndon has been variously described as "a little ragged village...to which abundance of people go in the season to drink the waters...but wretched lodging and entertainment" (18th century)*; a place with salubrious air, reputed to be one of the healthiest in the county - the roadsides lined with trees, and, all around, ... charming walks over hill and dale" (19th century)[†]; "a pleasant hillside village - the home of prosperous fugitives from Derby" (20th century)[#]; "a comfortable mixture of Georgian, Victorian and modern houses, mostly backing on to farmland" (21st century)[‡].

Quarndon has a population of 903. Since the boundary changes of 1984, 32 houses have been built in the village - including the Sulley's Field and Somme Road developments - bringing the current total to 379.

Photo: David Widdows

"A pleasant, hillside village...backing on to farmland"

---

*Daniel Defoe: *Tour Through the Whole Island of Great Britain*, 1727; [†]Bulmer's *History, Topography & Directory: Derbyshire*, 1895; [#]Roy Christian: *Derbyshire* (Batsford, 1978); [‡]Caroline Wheeler: *Derbyshire Life & Countryside*, May, 2001.

© 2008 Courtesy: Derby Museums & Art Gallery   Courtesy: The Curzon family

© Courtesy: Derby Local Studies Library

Quarndon's Chapel

Top: 19th century engraving and photograph (from Church Road). The building to the left of the West Tower may have been a School Room, or, more probably, part of the enlargement of the Chapel in 1835.

Bottom left: The path today. *Bottom centre:* The West Tower, after the demolition of the Nave. NB: The holes on either side of the archway indicate the former existence of a musicians' gallery. *Bottom right:* The Tower today!

2. Quarndon's Chapel

*(The Editor wishes to thank **the Rev'd WILLIAM BATES**, Priest-in-Charge, St Paul's, Quarndon, for his advice and assistance with this Chapter and acknowledges the historical research undertaken by **Dr TIM WOODS** in connection with this Chapter and Chapter 6.)*

WHILE a stranger to Quarndon could hardly pass through the village without noticing the late 19th century Parish Church of St Paul - strategically perched on the summit of a hill - evidence of any remains of its medieval predecessor - known as Quarndon Chapel - is almost entirely obscured by ivy and other foliage. You will find the old Churchyard and what is left of the Grade II-listed Chapel Bell Tower near the bottom of Church Road, on the east side, just before Old Vicarage Lane. The Chapel had a Norman door - sadly not preserved or incorporated into the new Church when the Chapel was partly demolished in 1873-4 - indicating that it was operating as a place of worship in the early 12th century.

According to William the Conqueror's *Domesday Book* (1086), large areas of land in Quarndon, Little Chester and Little Eaton supported two churches in Derby, staffed by colleges of canons. (A college comprised three or more canons, or priests, attached to a church to sing perpetual masses for the souls of the dead.)

In the reign of Henry I (1100-1135), the two colleges were joined together under All Saints' Church (now Derby Cathedral) with its canons also serving St Alkmund's Church in Derby and Quarndon's Chapel. Henry then "bestowed upon" the Dean of the (newly-built) Lincoln Cathedral All Saints' College and its lands. The lands in Quarndon thus became part of the Dean's estate under the Manor of Little Chester.

Originally, a priest from All Saints' would be sent to say Mass in its 'daughter' Chapel in Quarndon. But, in 1547, as part of the Dissolution of the Chantries Act (under which certain colleges, chapels, etc, and their possessions, "were given to the King's Majesty"), All Saints', Derby, and its satellites - Derby's St Alkmund's Church, Little Chester, Little Eaton and Quarndon's Chapel - came under attack.

As a result, under the Protestant King Edward VI, assets of All Saints' Church (worth £38 14s) - together with those of the six canons - were requisitioned by the Crown and sold for £346 13s 4d. (Only property held by the churchwardens for the repair of church fabric was spared.)

© Courtesy: Derby Local Studies Library

All Saints' Church, Derby, c. 1560. (Now Derby Cathedral)

5

The six canons were pensioned off, but no provision was made for the appointment and payment of a priest to conduct services. This left All Saints' - and Quarndon - stranded in terms of finance and the provision of clergy.

Edward VI died in 1553 and was succeeded by his Catholic half-sister, Mary I, who, two years later, came to the rescue of All Saints'. Having been petitioned by the burghers of Derby, she gave a large parcel of land in Little Chester - which, until 1547, had supported the canons financially - to the corporation of Derby to provide an income for two clergy to officiate at All Saints' and, by inference, Quarndon.

This could be seen as an astute move on the part of both Mary and the borough of Derby. Had she simply let the ownership of the land pass back to the Church, her Protestant half-sister, Elizabeth, could have reversed the arrangement when she came to the throne. But, in the custody of the burghers of Derby, the land was in safer hands. This was borne out in 1592 when Elizabeth I made grants of All Saints' land to a local landowner. Derby Corporation challenged the transaction, took the case to the Court of Exchequer and won the day for the Church!

Quarndon's Chapel, however, was never generously endowed. When the Royal Commissioner visited the Chapel at the time of the Reformation it contained little of value, having just two bells and one silver-gilt chalice.

© 2008 Courtesy: Derby Museums & Art Gallery

Top: **Chapel from SW.** *Bottom:* **Chapel from SE**

17th century papers show that a churchwarden for Quarndon was selected at the All Saints' vestry meeting. There were also frequent disputes between Quarndon Chapel and All Saints' over the fees it was having to pay towards the upkeep of the latter. In 1620 it was decided that Quarndon pay a tenth of the annual assessment. Then, 17 years later, when major repairs to the chancel of All Saints' became necessary, an argument over Quarndon's liability was put to arbitration. Eventually a compromise solution was reached: cancel any past debts and require Quarndon to pay half the cost of the chancel repairs. It's interesting to note, by the way, that for this judgement the arbitrators were remunerated in the form of "a quart" (1.136 litres) "of sack" (dry white wine), costing "1s 2d".

Quarndon Chapel had a small west tower and a short, four-sided, lead-covered spire. (Apparently, the only reason that the west tower and belfry were left standing when the rest of the building was demolished in 1873-4 was that they were so entwined with ivy!) The south doorway was Norman and there was a small, blocked-up priest's door. Around 1800, before Gothic features became fashionable, the Chapel was largely rebuilt with good quality stonework and box pews. A musicians' gallery was also built into the west end, and, at the east end, there was, unusually, a stone altar.

In 1677, Adrian Mundy, a churchwarden who owned a mansion (*Old Quarndon Hall* - demolished by Lord Scarsdale in 1812 - see Chapter 1) on what is now Old Vicarage Lane, left an endowment of £3 "to be employed towards the living of a minister to read divine service at the chapel". But if there were no minister, the money was to be divided amongst the poor.

In 1697, at the height of Quarndon's prosperity as a 'spa' village (see Chapter 10), the Bishop of Lichfield and Coventry wrote to the authorities complaining that services were of "a very desultory nature" and directed that there should be a service in the Chapel every Sunday in the summer months. As a result, 16 clergy were designated to share the duty.

Quarndon didn't become a separate parish until 1736. The marriage register begins in 1755, baptisms are registered from 1772 and the churchyard wasn't consecrated for burials until 1821.

Former Norman door

Thomas Manlove, incumbent from 1762 to 1802, was both Vicar of St Alkmund's, Derby, and Curate of Quarndon in plurality (receiving the income from both). However, when he was expected to take Sunday services in Quarndon, he gave up his curacy! In fact in 1793, when Quarndon parish became eligible for £200 from Queen Anne's Bounty (a fund established in 1704 to help poorer clergy), this was declined because Manlove refused to accede to the condition that "he do duty in the Chapel once every Sunday"!

A continuing lack of funds was another reason for the delay in appointing an incumbent solely for Quarndon. A vicar needs a vicarage and vicarages cost money! So we find responsibility for the Chapel passing from All Saints', Derby, to St Alkmund's, Derby, and then to St Alkmund's, Duffield. In 1824, for instance, the 'perpetual curate' for

Quarndon was William Barber. His main income of £149 a year came from being Vicar of Duffield, with Quarndon providing £46 a year. This was not a generous income, but Barber lived in his vicarage in Duffield. His curate lived in Derby, so, again, there was no need for a parsonage. But, two decades later, Joseph Humpstone of Derby "gave £1,000 in 3% Consols for the support of a resident minister, on condition that the Church Building Society erects a parsonage". This it duly did in 1844, east of the old churchyard (see *right*), at a cost of £850. It was occupied as a *Vicarage* until the new *Vicarage* on Church Road was built in 1935. *The Old Vicarage* is now a private house.

The Old Vicarage

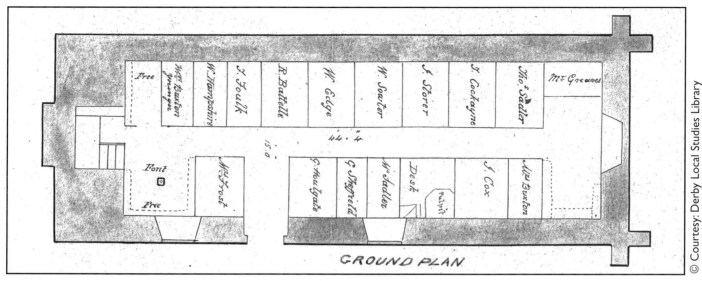

© Courtesy: Derby Local Studies Library

Ground plan of 1825

Memorial stones in old Churchyard

The Chapel was enlarged in 1835, but it remained small. Estimates of the number of people it accommodated range from 150 to 200 - which seems optimistic. In 1851 Sunday attendance was about 102 in the morning and 98 in the afternoon - plus Sunday School in the morning and afternoon, about 50 children attending each. (Corresponding figures for 2007/8 are given in Chapter 19.)

In the early 1960s a group of volunteers widened the entrance, levelled and grassed the old churchyard and laid out the memorial stones.

Old Chapel interior
The text over the altar would have read:
"Glory to God in the highest".

3. Quarndon's Mill

ONE of the most important industrial features of medieval Quarndon must have been its 12th century Water Mill - first mentioned in the Charters of Roger de Rolveston, Dean of Lincoln from 1195 until 1223, when he granted part of Querndon Mill to William Rolveston at 12 pence per annum. You will find the site of the Mill in the field behind *Tamaris* (a private house) at the bottom of Old Vicarage Lane.

Photo: Derek Wigley

Former house on site

Our picture shows a house - re-built in the 17th century, but now demolished - which stood on the site of *Tamaris* and may have looked like the original Mill House. According to Derek Wigley, the centre - where the roof has collapsed - would have had no floor between ground and ceiling and access to the upper rooms at each end would have been by ladder.

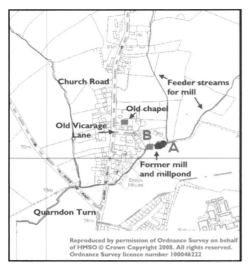

Map of Mill area
Matthew Pitt

Confluence of two streams (From Point A on map)

The site of the Mill is a very flat field. According to Frank Stone (a major source of information for this book): "Garden parties, children's sports and festivities celebrating George V's Silver Jubilee in 1935 were held there." The mill stream runs along the south side of the field (on its way to the Markeaton Brook) and, if you cross the stile on the east side, you will see how the confluence of two streams - one from the north, another from the north-east - creates the mill stream. A 'head' of water would have been formed by a series of sluices, but, because of the shallowness of the stream, the Mill was probably powered by an under-shot wheel, where, instead of driving it from the top, the water struck the wheel from the bottom.

It is thought that the Mill may have fallen into disuse following the Black Death of 1348-51, which wiped out a third of this country's population. What we do know is that a Manor Court ruling 200 years later stated that the inhabitants of Quarndon must take their grain to Little Eaton for milling.

Mill pond field (From Point B on map)

Drawing by Chris Frith

Diagram of 'under-shot' mill-wheel

4. Burley Hill Pottery

(The Editor thanks JONATHAN WALLIS, Principal Curator, Collections, Derby Museums & Art Gallery, PAT TINKLER and ROY HUGHES for their assistance with this chapter.)

QUESTION: What do horseshoes, 'thumb pie-crusting', an attic sale and a World War 2 tank have in common? The answer lies at the bottom of Burley Lane. In January, 1862, while drainage work was being carried out by the Kedleston Estate on its field on the right before you reach the Duffield Road, fragments of pots were unearthed. This led to the discovery of a site, which, between 1250 and 1375, had produced what is known as **Burley Hill Pottery.** An account of this historic find is given in detail in *The Ceramic Art of Great Britain*, published in 1878, by the archaeologist, Llewellyn Jewitt.

The earliest reference to a pottery at Burley is in a collection of 12th to 14th century charters (formal documents conferring rights or liberties), which refer to grants of land made by local landowners to the newly-founded Darley Abbey. In the mid 13th century, "half an acre in the fields of Burley, which Alan the Potter held," was granted by William, son of Peter of Burley, to the Abbey Canons.

Plate 1

Plate 1 shows engravings of Burley Hill pottery from Llewellyn Jewitt's book. They should be compared with Plate 2, illustrating actual Burley Hill pottery sold by the executors of the 3rd Viscount Scarsdale and the Curzon family at an Attic Sale at *Kedleston Hall* on 13th March, 2002. In their catalogue, Neales, the auctioneers, described the pot *third* from *left* in Plate 1 and *fourth* from *left* in Plate 2 as "a rare medieval Burley Hill pottery jug of tapering cylindrical form, beneath a tall, spool-shaped neck and loop handle; degraded lead glaze; 7 inches high". The pot *third* from *left* in Plate 2 is obviously the one on the *left* in Plate 1.

Plate 2

Jewitt called the 1862 excavations "the only instance of finding a kiln either of Anglo-Saxon or Norman periods" and described the pots as "highly interesting vessels, or fragments of vessels...in a reddish clay and partially glazed". He adds that they were "in potter's parlance, 'wasters' - ie, 'fire-cracked', 'run' or otherwise spoiled in the firing ... The discovery is one of great historical importance and it is fortunate that it has been made on the estate of a nobleman who knows how to appreciate its value." 140 years later, at the Attic Sale, the pots illustrated in Plate 2 fetched a total of £3,525!

Photo: Pat Tinkler

Plate 3
Burley Hill pitcher, with horseshoe motif, which remains at *Kedleston Hall*

© 2008 Courtesy: Derby Museums & Art Gallery

Plate 4

In 1957 the Burley Hill site was rediscovered. But those engaged in the excavations were astonished at how small the fragments were - until they discovered that the area had been requisitioned as a testing ground for the Cromwell tank in World War 2! (See Chapter 30.)

On the north side of Burley Lane is what looks distinctly like a man-made hill, which could have been the potter's dumping heap. Harold Coulthread (who writes on *Burley Grange Farm* in Chapter 8) says that his tractor often turned up fragments of fired clay in the area.

Plate 4 shows the display in Derby's Museum & Art Gallery of pots from the 1957 excavation. The caption on the display cabinet reads: "The products of this important pottery (the only known pottery site in the south of Derbyshire) have been known for very much longer than the exact site of manufacture. The kilns were coal-fired and the pottery can be both glazed and unglazed. The commoner, glazed ware has a light to dark green glaze. Decoration took the form of clay pods, modelled into leaves, flowers" (see *third* from *left*), "buckles, human faces, ribbons of clay with thumb 'pie-crusting' and horseshoes" (see *second* from *left*).

Plate 3, *opposite*, shows a pitcher with horseshoe decoration, which was not included in the Attic Sale at *Kedleston Hall*.

As Jewitt pointed out: "The horseshoe is the distinctive bearing of the family of de Ferrers (Earls of Ferrers, of Derby and Nottingham), who held Duffield Castle from the time of the Norman Conquest to the reign of Henry III, when the lands were confiscated." At the time of publication, the Derbyshire Archaeological Society has been excavating the site in search of remains of the actual kiln. So far, none has been found.

BUNKERS HILL, NEAR DERBY

Courtesy: Rod Jewell Collection

Photo: David Widdows

Bunkers Hill

Top: Picnicking in the 19th century. *Bottom:* The hill today

5. Bunkers Hill

OVER the years, Bunkers Hill has been the scene of much celebrating and commemorating, not least at the Unveiling of a Millennium Topograph & Seat in September, 2001 (see Chapter 32) - permission to erect them there having been granted by the 3ʳᵈ Viscount Scarsdale before his death the previous year. But where the Hill got its name from (sometimes spelt on maps 'Bunker's; sometimes without the apostrophe) is - as with Quarndon - far from clear.

Brian Rich, of Keele University's Centre for Continuing & Professional Education, points out that places like Bunkers Hill, which are on the edges of settlements or villages (until the boundary changes of 1984, Bunkers Hill was on the outskirts of Duffield) are sometimes given the 'borrowed' name of a far-off country or location - like 'California', 'New Zealand' or 'World's End'. He cites as a local example that in a map of 1860, the present *Botany Farm* - again in a remote spot - was originally called "*Botany Bay Farm*".

So is Quarndon's Bunkers Hill named after Bunker (ie, no final 's') Hill outside Boston, Massachusetts - scene of the battle of that name in 1775, when the colonial forces, faced with the oncoming British Army, were given the order: "Hold your fire till you see the whites of their eyes!"? The battlefield is certainly on the edge of a settlement, being described as "an ancient moraine, an isthmus, running out into Boston Bay, almost like a causeway, on which rise three little oval hills (geologically 'drumlins') of which Bunker Hill is one".

The Topograph on Bunkers Hill

As the writer of the "Notes & Queries" column in the *Derbyshire Advertiser* of 3rd August, 1945, put it: "I have always assumed that Bunkers Hill of the Quarndon district was copied from the American example." But there are other theories. Included among definitions of "bunker" in the *Oxford English Dictionary* are "a receptacle for coal or coke", "a sandy hollow (golf)", "a military dug-out or reinforced shelter" and "a seat or bench (serving also for a chest); an earthen seat or bank in the fields".

A geological map (*Ordnance Survey*, 1955) of the area labels it as "soft, pale, brown cross-bedded, coarse-grained pebbly sandstone. WORKED FOR GRAVEL", and we know from the ledgers of the Surveyors of the Highways that, between 1792 and 1818, 5,300 wagon loads of gravel and shale were taken from Bunkers Hill (south of the summit) to build the village roads. This would therefore partly account for the number of hollows, or bunkers, to be found there.

South of the Hill is a field called Stonepit Close; to the east is another called Brick Kiln Close. This would imply that clay from the vicinity - as well as being used by Burley Hill Pottery (see Chapter 4) - was mixed with pebbles and fired with fuel from neighbouring Burley Wood to make bricks. (As is illustrated in Chapter 12, a characteristic of Quarndon bricks is that they are indeed embedded with pebbles.)

Previously, Bunkers Hill was called "Oaklea Moor". Maybe the change of name took place because of the extracting. We also know from an eye witness (Roland Darvell, an evacuee to Quarndon, see Chapter 29) that, early in World War 2, a German bomb was dropped on Bunkers Hill, leaving a huge crater.

It is also possible that, at some point, the Hill was used as a fort. In his MA thesis, *Facets of Enclosure*, Noel Tornbohm writes: "Next to Stonepit Close is a field called Hill Close. This enjoys a commanding position looking out over the Derwent valley with uninterrupted views for many kilometres to the north, south and east. It is at the top of a steep rise, some 100 metres above the river, making it an ideal position for a hill fort. Beighton's *1763 Survey* [see below] shows a horseshoe-shaped feature that could represent fortifications. (The map is likely to have been drawn before the field was disturbed for other purposes.)"

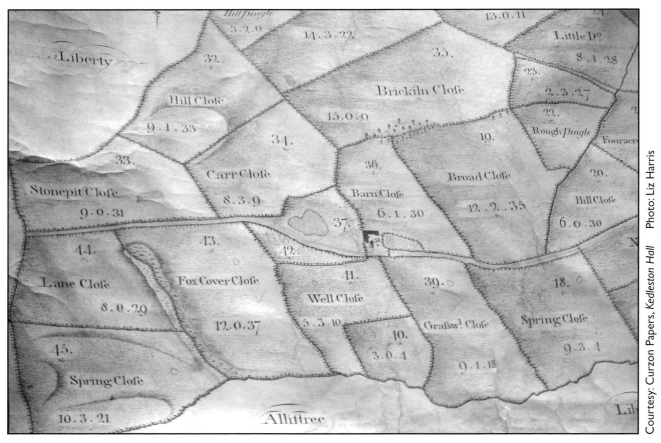

Horseshoe shape (*top left*) in Hill Close (Bunkers Hill). To help you locate the fields, *Burley Grange Farm* is in Barn Close (field number 36 in *centre* of map). NB: Not to be confused with Barn Close in the middle of the village!

The Hill was a favourite spot for picnics in the 19th and early 20th centuries. Ivan Cope recalled that "when children rolled down the slope they ended up black as soot". It is also said that bonfires blazed on Bunkers Hill to commemorate Queen Victoria's Golden Jubilee in 1887. According to Frank Stone: "Originally, two large beech trees marked the summit and were a distinctive landmark from many miles around. Unfortunately, they both blew down during a gale in the mid-1930s." He also adds that a bonfire was lit on the Hill to celebrate Queen Elizabeth II's Silver Jubilee in 1977.

From the summit, the view is very little changed from the one Edward Bradbury, the *Derbyshire Advertiser* columnist, described in July, 1928:

> "Let us rest awhile on the breezy summit while the panorama of it photographs itself on our memory...The valley of the Derwent is spread before us: the Chevin spur of upland, the Little Eaton heights, the wooded slopes of Duffield bank, the Duffield church - close by the river, which gleams in the sun like liquid light - and the Midland Railway, with rushing expresses and rumbling goods trains, disappearing in Milford Tunnel."

Photo: Don Hall

The "panorama" from "the breezy summit".

Stone House Prebend
(Old Chester Road, Chester Green)
**The stone chimney stacks date back to Medieval times when the building was part of a
prebendal* estate. (*Explained on *opposite page*).**

6. Village law, order & government

*In this chapter, all key officers and public bodies and buildings are printed in **bold type**.*

By NOEL TORNBOHM, LINDA OWEN & BRYAN HARRIS

IN Medieval England, all land was deemed to belong to the **KING**, but in many cases he leased it to noblemen - known as **TENANTS-IN-CHIEF** - in return for services (originally military ones). He kept some land for himself, which included much of Derby - to which was attached land at Little Chester (including the modern Chester Green).

The land acquired by the nobles was divided into small estates called **Manors**. These were usually sub-let to local gentry, who were known as **Lords of the Manor**, and it was to them that the villagers - depending on their status - were required to provide such services as ploughing and harvest-gathering.

Many manors in Derbyshire were arranged in groups of three, with a principal and two subsidiary manors. This was the case with **Quarndon**, which, together with **Little Eaton**, was a subsidiary, or "outlier", of **Little Chester**. The function of the outliers was to grow staple crops, and, after feeding themselves, to forward the surplus to the principal manor for the use of the lord. (A similar arrangement existed in neighbouring Markeaton, with outliers in Mackworth and Allestree.)

Quarndon's early community grew up in and around the area of what became the estate of *Quarndon Old Hall*, which (as is explained in Chapter 1) stood in the vicinity of the present Old Vicarage Lane, but was demolished in 1812. Here the inhabitants grew crops for the principal manor of Little Chester.

But, as is explained in Chapter 2, between 1100 and 1109, the manors of Quarndon, Little Chester and Little Eaton - which then belonged to **All Saints' College of Canons** in **Derby** - were 'gifted' to **Lincoln Cathedral** by **Henry I**. Thus successive **Deans** of Lincoln became lords of these manors, with each of the College Canons (prebendaries) being allocated a piece of farmland (prebend - from Medieval Latin: *praebenda*, meaning pension) from which to draw his income. This farmland existed in Little Chester, with additional land in Quarndon and Little Eaton. Illustrated on the opposite page is *Stone House Prebend*, Chester Green, where the Medieval stone chimney stacks date back to the time when the building was part of a prebendal estate.

As is also explained in Chapter 2, the College of Canons was closed under the Dissolution of the Chantries Act (1547-8), but provision was later made by Mary I to ensure that ownership of the displaced Canons' former lands protected them for the rest of their lives. From this time, until 1865, the Manor of Quarndon was held by successive leaseholders - the last being the Dukes of Devonshire from 1764 to 1865. After that, the land was gradually sold.

In the first half of the eighteenth century the **Curzon** family - owners of *Kedleston Hall* and **Park** (with the head of the family being lord of the manor of Kedleston) - purchased much of Quarndon and the surrounding area - thus creating a large estate.

So how did it all work?

Pinfold Cottage & Wall, 1980s

The same view at the time of publication

For centuries most people who lived in villages were dependent on the lord of the manor for their livelihoods. He would usually employ a **Steward**, or **Bailiff**, who would not only act as his link with his tenants, but would also preside at meetings of the **Manorial Court**. This would be held every two or three weeks - in Quarndon's case at Little Chester - and at it would sit a 12-man **Manor Court Jury**. All tenants were obliged to attend the Court unless they could show "just cause" to stay away. Twice a year, another court was held at which representatives (usually four) were chosen to attend the more important **Hundred** (district) **Court**.

Manorial officers included the **Reeve**, **Greave** or **Grave**, who was elected by his fellow-tenants as the intermediary between themselves and the lord of the manor - becoming, in effect, the 'head man'.

The **Hayward** was responsible for the maintenance of hedges and fences to prevent cattle from straying.

But if cattle did stray the **Village Pinder** or **Pounder** was an official employed by the Manor Court to round them up and impound them in a **Pinfold**. These were necessary before the enclosures acts, when much of the countryside was unfenced, or inadequately so, and straying animals could cause considerable damage. The offending creature, if caught, would only be released to its owner (who would also have to pay compensation for any damage caused) on payment of a fine - probably one penny.

Quarndon's Pinfold was at 226 Burley Lane - *Pinfold Cottage* (see *above*). The house was extended in the year 2000, but the **Pinfold Wall** was preserved.

Remains of local pinfolds exist in Hazelwood, Farnah Green, Hope, Egginton, Barrow-on-Trent, Hathersage and Sandiacre.

In each **Shire** or **County** the most important officer was the **Sheriff** (or "Shire-reeve"). He carried out the orders of the king and was responsible for keeping order and for receiving the King's **Judges** when they came to preside in Court. From 1361 onwards **Justices of the Peace** were appointed to maintain order - selected exclusively from the local gentry. Chief among these was the **Lord Lieutenant**, whose duty was also to raise and lead the local **Militia** (members of the civilian population who were required to take up arms in times of national emergency).

As regards the way villages were **governed**, we need to go back to 7th century England, when the **Church** divided the country into **parishes** - the official business of each parish being carried out by a **Vestry**, which organised local rates and charities and appointed a team of parish officials.

Church Wardens (an ancient, unpaid post) were responsible for the care of church buildings, managing church estates and providing everything necessary for church services. They also gave relief to the itinerant poor and paid the bell ringers.

The Parish Clerk (which originated in the 17th century and was an office for life) was paid from church funds. He was expected to assist the parish priest, ring the bells, sweep out the church and wash the priest's surplices.

But gradually over the years - particularly after the reign of Henry VIII - parishes took on an increasing role in the civil governance and conduct of village life.

The **Parish Constable** dealt with petty law and order. He was responsible for the **stocks**, the **pillory**, the parish **lock-up**, **weights and measures** and the supervision of **ale-houses**. He collected the **Poll Tax**, **Hearth Tax** and **Land Tax** and he escorted prisoners to the **Assizes** and **Quarter Sessions**. When required, he raised the local militia and lit the **beacon** (in Quarndon's case on Bunkers Hill). This was an annual appointment and was usually shared on rotation between more affluent members of the community, such as farmers and craftsmen. In some areas, the constable was known as the **Beadle** (eg, Bumble in Charles Dickens's *Oliver Twist*); in others, the beadle was the **Constable's Assistant**.

The **Surveyor of the Highways** could raise taxes and was expected to supervise labourers maintaining local roads. (Quarndon's Highways Accounts show that women were employed on the roads as stone-pickers.)

The **Overseer of the Poor** was allowed to raise taxes in order to meet the demands of poor relief. Much of his time would be spent ascertaining who would be a burden on the parish finances and, where appropriate, returning them to the parish to which they belonged. His other responsibilities included apprenticing poor orphans to local householders, selling passes to strangers travelling through the village, paying the parish constable and clerk and identifying and bringing to account the fathers of illegitimate children.

The Quarndon accounts from the early part of the 19th century show the Overseer "paying George Fearn's rent (£1 10s) and the costs of burying his wife (£1 11s 6d)"; "pass for man, wife & 4 children (1s)"; "new clarinet (£1 4s) and bell ropes (4s 9d) for Chapel"; "Liddy Cadman for picking stones (2s)"; "pair of handcuffs for constable (2s 6d)"; "leeches for Dorothy Fowke when ill (3s)", "box of coal for Old Nanny Fowke (15s)"; "to the examination and swearing of Sarah Cadman to the father of her child (5s)" and "to the journey to meet John Payne to get his bond for Sarah Cadman's child (2s)" - thus ensuring that the maintenance of the child passed from the parish to the father.

The history of poor relief goes back to Tudor times. Until the reign of Henry VIII, monks and nuns had cared for the poor in their area. But, after the Dissolution of the Monasteries, the responsibility passed to the inhabitants of each parish. Laws were introduced to set up funds providing financial assistance for the old, training in a trade for children and work for beggars. The burden of these payments fell on the owners of property, but, over the centuries, very little reform of these laws took place, so that, come the Industrial Revolution, manufacturers in towns took on workmen from the villages in the good times, then sent them back, unsupported, when work was scarce.

Babington Workhouse (Now Hospital)

In 1834 a new **Poor Law** was passed, based on the belief that providing poor people with money encouraged laziness. A **Poor Law Board** was established, followed by a nationwide increase in the building of **workhouses**, with the ultimate intention that the harsh conditions experienced in these institutions would goad the inmates into seeking work outside.

This also relieved the parishes of much of their responsibility to the poor, some of whom might be living rough in the fields, receiving **Parish Outdoor Relief**. **Hiring Fairs** were organised to place people into work.

Quarndon's poor were originally sent to Shardlow Workhouse, but, later, parishes were grouped into a Union, thus reducing the duplication of services and thereby saving the parishes money.

Quarndon, along with 32 other parishes, was placed in the **Belper Union** - its poor and unemployed being sent to **Babington Workhouse** (see *left*). Money to support these institutions was collected by the Overseer.

In 1908 the **Old Age Pensions Act** greatly reduced both the poverty of the elderly and the need for the Overseer to collect money for the workhouse. Quarndon Parish Council minutes record that in September, 1909, there were "no paupers in the Workhouse from this Parish".

The role of the Overseer would probably have disappeared around this time but for the outbreak of World War I in 1914. However, in 1921, the passing of the **Local Government Act** led eventually to the abolition of the post - its duties, such as they were, being taken over, first by **Public Assistance Committees** and subsequently by the **Social Services Department**.

As regards **elections** and **voting rights**, prior to 1832 very few villagers were entitled to vote in **parliamentary elections**. But those who did have the right had to swear openly the name of the candidate that they wished to vote for - the voter generally choosing the candidate that his landlord had put forward, even if it was against his better judgement!

Even as late as 1835 the Government published a *List of Electors for the Southern Division of the County of Derby, showing how they voted at the Contested Election, January 20th & 21st, 1835*. It names the candidates (without identifying their political parties) as: Sir Roger Greisley, Bart, Sir George Crewe, Bart, the Hon. G. J. Vernon and the Rt Hon. Lord Waterpark. In the facsimile reproduced on the following page you will see that each candidate is identified at the top of his column by the initial letter of his surname.

The votes cast by the 18 Quarndon voters (two per voter) are indicated by a horizontal line. However, under later Reform Acts, the franchise was widened, leading to the introduction of the **secret ballot**.

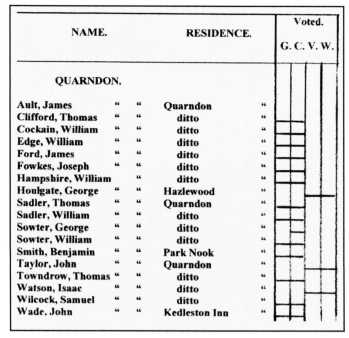

NAME.	RESIDENCE.	Voted. G. C. V. W.
QUARNDON.		
Ault, James " "	Quarndon "	
Clifford, Thomas " "	ditto "	
Cockain, William " "	ditto "	
Edge, William " "	ditto "	
Ford, James " "	ditto "	
Fowkes, Joseph " "	ditto "	
Hampshire, William "	ditto "	
Houlgate, George " "	Hazlewood "	
Sadler, Thomas " "	Quarndon "	
Sadler, William " "	ditto "	
Sowter, George " "	ditto "	
Sowter, William " "	ditto "	
Smith, Benjamin " "	Park Nook "	
Taylor, John " "	Quarndon "	
Towndrow, Thomas " "	ditto "	
Watson, Isaac " "	ditto "	
Wilcock, Samuel " "	ditto "	
Wade, John " "	Kedleston Inn "	

Voting record

In 1888, **County Councils**, with elected members, were established. Then 1894 saw the introduction of **Rural District Councils**, including **Belper RDC** (which covered Quarndon). This was inherited by **Amber Valley District Council** in 1974, adopting the title **Borough Council** in 1989.

County Councils are responsible for education, social services, libraries, museums, bus services, planning policy, highways, traffic control, refuse disposal and nominating members to the local police and fire authorities.

District or **Borough Councils** look after local planning, environmental health, refuse collection, clean air, parks, playing fields, swimming baths and housing policy - though most of them have sold off their housing stock to (non-profit-making) housing companies.

Quarndon became an **Ecclesiastical Parish** in 1736, but, under the Local Government Act of 1894, **ecclesiastical rural parishes with more than 300 electors** also became **Civil** parishes, run by a **Parish Council**. The same year, **Quarndon's** first **Parish Meeting** was held on 4th December, followed by its first **Parish Council Meeting** on 13th December. This had **five members**. Today's Parish Council has **nine** members and employs a part-time **Clerk**.

The duties of a **Parish Council** include commenting on planning applications; the maintenance of bus shelters and road lighting; crime prevention, litter bins and the inspection of public footpaths and bridleways; supporting tourism, traffic calming, bus services and police authorities; investigating the needs of local road and transport services and publicising local library services.

In Quarndon's case it also looks after the **Millennium Topograph & Seat**, the **Jubilee Seat**, the **Human Sun Clock**, the **Church Clock**, the **Chalybeate Well**, the **Barn Close Children's Play Area** and the **Village Hall Car Park**.

Today Quarndon is in the **Duffield Division** of **Derbyshire County Council** and the **South West Parishes Ward** of **Amber Valley Borough Council**. At the time of publication, it is in the **West Derbyshire Constituency** in **Parliamentary Elections**, but, under boundary changes which will apply from the next General Election, the constituency will be split up, with Belper and Duffield going into a new seat called **Mid-Derbyshire** and Quarndon becoming part of another new seat called **Derbyshire Dales**. Quarndon is also in the **East Midlands Constituency** of the **European Parliament**.

In 1989 Derby City Council proposed to the Boundaries Commission that its borders should be extended to include Quarndon. At a public meeting in the Village Hall this was opposed by 141 votes, with none in favour and one abstention. The Commission rejected the proposal.

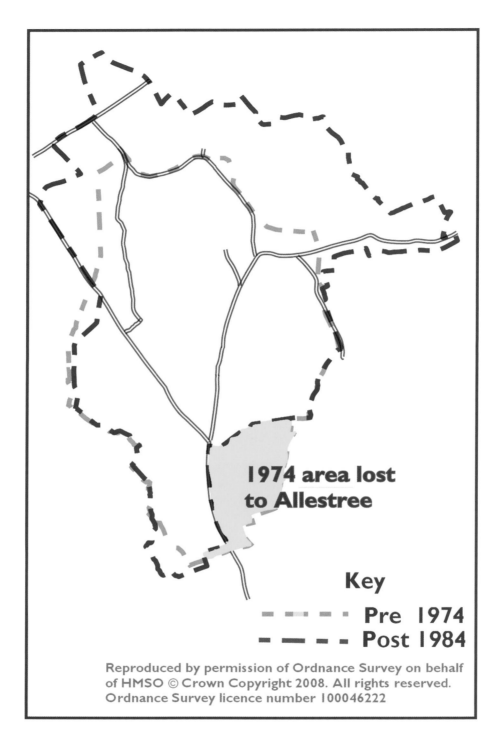

Key

␣␣␣␣ Pre 1974
━ ━ ━ Post 1984

Reproduced by permission of Ordnance Survey on behalf of HMSO © Crown Copyright 2008. All rights reserved. Ordnance Survey licence number 100046222

Quarndon's boundaries
Map by Matthew Pitt

7. Boundaries, roads & turnpikes

By *MATTHEW PITT & BRYAN HARRIS*

THE story of boundaries is much more interesting than the rather dry topic one might expect. Boundaries are forever changing to suit different circumstances. Having some understanding of parish boundaries, for instance, is important for anyone doing research into family history. Births, marriages and deaths were registered by parish and it is often important to know in which parish a place was at a particular time.

As is explained in Chapter 6, a **manor** of Quarndon, with a lord of the manor, has existed for over a thousand years. And, as is explained in Chapter 2, an **ecclesiastical parish** of Quarndon has existed since 1736. But, as is also explained in Chapter 6, under the 1894 Local Government Act, **ecclesiastical** rural parishes with more than 300 electors also became **civil** parishes, run by a **parish council**.

On the map on the *opposite page*, the **red** line shows the Quarndon boundary **pre-1974**. But, in that year, Derby expanded and Quarndon lost an area around Woodlands School to Allestree. This area is coloured **yellow.**

Then, in 1984, there was a change in parish boundaries within Amber Valley. Quarndon gained significant areas to the north from Duffield, Weston Underwood and Kedleston. For example, much of Burley Lane and the area to the north of The Common were transferred from Duffield to Quarndon. There was also a change to the Quarndon-Kedleston boundary along the Kedleston Road near the Golf Course. The **1984** boundary is marked in **blue**.

Regarding the **civil & ecclesiastical** division, since 1974 those living in the **yellow** area taken over by Derby that year, while being parishioners of St Paul's Church, Quarndon, are residents of **Allestree** (in Derby), not Quarndon. The **civil** parish of Quarndon is that within the **blue** line; the **ecclesiastical** parish is that within the **blue** line, plus the **yellow** area.

Until 1984 Quarndon's boundary with Duffield was on the brow of Burley Lane, west of *Holmwood*. It went north, then bore left through the footpath behind Montpelier and came out on The Common, so that *Quarndon House, The Elms, Quarndon Hill* and *Fernhill* were all in **Duffield**.

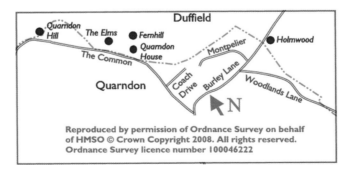

Reproduced by permission of Ordnance Survey on behalf of HMSO © Crown Copyright 2008. All rights reserved. Ordnance Survey licence number 100046222

Detail - by Matthew Pitt - showing pre-1984 boundary in red, as it affected a section of The Common

Vine Cottage

Battelles Lane

Over the centuries the road layout in and around Quarndon has changed significantly. In the early days there was a main road from the south, but most of the roads (or tracks as they would have been) largely went east-west.

Quarndon was on the route from Mackworth (where the 15th century Castle Gatehouse still stands) to Breadsall, passing through Hunter's Gully (see *opposite page*), which leads from Quarndon Turn (at the southern village boundary) to the present Woodlands School.

A track following the stream as it runs from the former Mill to the Markeaton Brook crossed Quarndon Turn, where the stream is culverted. As evidence of this, a mounting block still exists in the field between Church Road and Kedleston Road (see *opposite page*).

There was also a track going west, which joined the old road leading towards Kedleston. There would also have been many other local tracks used for farming and transporting materials.

There is evidence of an old road from Derby which came north, close to Park Farm, and then followed a ridge east of Kedleston Road and down towards Quarndon near the Old Mill - hence the former Toll House, now *Brook Cottage* (see *opposite page*) off Old Vicarage Lane. Some of these early tracks have been obliterated by turnpikes and the building of Allestree and Quarndon, but some remain as footpaths.

Until the 17th century the majority of travel took the form of walking or riding, but improvements in roads were urgently needed to cope with the increase in wheeled vehicles - particularly carriages. The solution was to set up turnpikes (toll roads), with toll houses being erected to collect the payments. One of these turnpikes was Battelles Lane (see *opposite & above*) - now a bridle path leading from *Vine Cottage* on Church Road to *The Kedleston Hotel*. Today it's difficult to imagine a coach and horses negotiating such a narrow thoroughfare!

Photos: David Widdows

Hunter's Gully

Brook Cottage **(former Toll House)**

Photo: Liz Harris

Old track via
Battelles Lane
to North and West

Mounting
block

Site of mill
Brook Cottage

Old track from
Mackworth

Quarndon Turn

Old track via Hunter's
Gully to Allestree

Key

old tracks

current roads

Reproduced by permission of Ordnance Survey on behalf of HMSO © Crown
Copyright 2008. All rights reserved. Ordnance Survey licence number 100046222

Left: **Map, by Matthew Pitt, of former tracks (including Hunter's Gully) and positions of** *Brook Cottage* **(former Toll House) & Battelles Lane.** *Right:* **Mounting block.**

27

Photo: Don Hall

Willington Bridge Turnpike

The word "turnpike" referred originally to the barrier with revolving spikes which was installed as a toll-bar (see Willington Bridge example *above*), but eventually the word came to refer to the road itself.

The first turnpike to be improved in Derbyshire was a section of the London to Manchester highway under an Act of 1738. This passed through Derby, Quarndon, Kedleston, Mugginton and Hognaston, en route to Brassington.

From Derby the route - shown in **yellow** on the map *opposite* - followed the line of the present Kedleston Road up to Daisy Bank (almost opposite Derby University) and then ran west of the present Kedleston Road, past the former *Markeaton Hall*. This route is now the bridleway which runs from Markeaton Lane - near the bridge over the Markeaton Brook - past *Markeaton Stones*, until it reaches the bridleway leading to *Upper Vicarwood Farm*. From there, keeping to the west side of the Markeaton Brook, it passed to the old *Kedleston Hall* (the turnpike here is now obliterated) and continued in front of the Hall through Kedleston Park towards Mugginton, Weston Underwood, Hulland Ward and Brassington.

The turnpike also had a diversion via Quarndon - shown in **blue** - which went from Daisy Bank up the present line of Kedleston Road, past Quarndon's Chapel, the former Mill and Toll House, up to *Vine Cottage*, where it turned left into Battelles Lane to join up with the present Inn Lane. The route then continued up Inn Lane, turning left past (the present) *Beech Avenue Cottages* up to Cumberhills Road, where it turned left on to a road which continued to Mugginton.

But, in 1760, Sir Nathaniel Curzon, 5th Baronet and an MP, obtained by Act of Parliament the "doing away" of the old (**yellow**) turnpike road - which passed in front, not only of the old *Kedleston Hall*, but also of the *Rectory* and the small village of Kedleston - providing he made a road from Quarndon Turn to join the existing road to Weston Underwood and Mercaston. This **new** turnpike - shown in **red** - did, as required, start at Quarndon Turn, then followed a riding avenue known as "All Saints' Walk". On this, Sir Nathaniel sited his *New Inn* - now The *Kedleston Hotel & Restaurant* (a short link road by the *Inn* providing access to Inn Lane). The new turnpike then continued, at Sir Nathaniel's insistence, well away from *Kedleston Hall* and outside Kedleston Park, in a north-west direction, past the North Gate of the Park, to form the present junction with Cumberhills Road.

Incidentally, the re-siting of this turnpike necessitated the relocation - brick by brick - of *Kedleston Rectory* and all the Kedleston cottages!

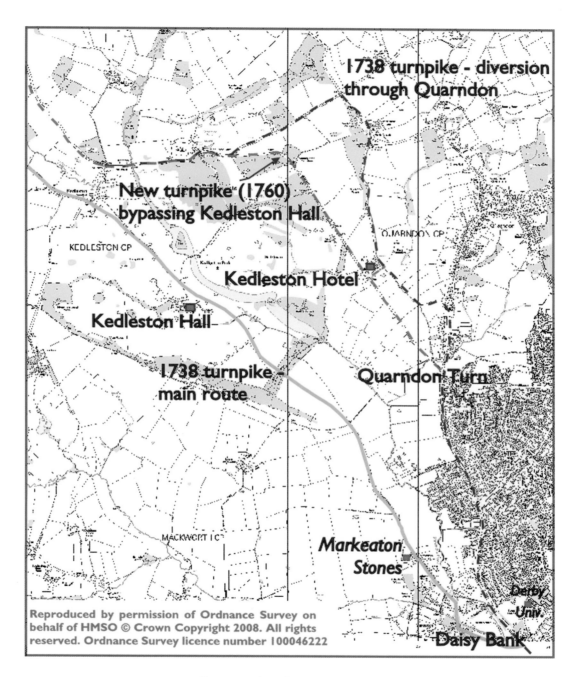

Labels on map:
1738 turnpike - diversion through Quarndon

New turnpike (1760) bypassing Kedleston Hall

Kedleston Hotel

Kedleston Hall

1738 turnpike - main route

Quarndon Turn

Markeaton Stones

Daisy Bank

Reproduced by permission of Ordnance Survey on behalf of HMSO © Crown Copyright 2008. All rights reserved. Ordnance Survey licence number 100046222

Quarndon's Turnpikes

Map by Matthew Pitt, showing the re-location of the 1738 turnpike (——) to the new route (– – – –) in 1760 - by-passing *Kedleston Hall*; also showing turnpike diversion (– – – –) through Quarndon, via Battelles Lane, Inn Lane & Cumberhills Road.

Since the 1760 turnpike was completed, the road layout has changed very little. However, some minor roads have closed and others have become footpaths or bridleways - for example, the old roads across to Allestree and Duffield are now footpaths.

Between March, 1759, and October, 1760, much of the stone to build *Kedleston Hall* was conveyed by wagoners - probably by sledge, drawn by twelve horses - having been quarried from the remains of King John's Horsley Castle (also known as Horston or Horiston) at Coxbench. The route is thought to have been over Duffield Bridge (by *The Bridge Inn*), across the present A6 and up a pack-horse way through Burley Wood (west of Bunkers Hill), joining up with what is now the top end of Woodlands Lane and then down through the village to Kedleston Park. Ledgers in the archives at *Kedleston Hall* show that, on average, 30 or 40 cubic feet of stone were being transported daily (sometimes involving five different loads) - the figure for the month of September, 1759, alone being over 4,000 cubic feet of stone at a cost of £84. (Other stone for the *Hall* was quarried from Langley, Chevin, Duffield, Morley Moor, Haywood and Hopton Wood.)

As you'll see from the sketch map below, the names of all the roads in Quarndon have changed since 1817:

Allestree Road is now Woodlands Lane.

Park Nook Road is now The Common & the north end of Church Road.

Duffield Road is now Burley Lane.

Park Lane Road is now Inn Lane.

Ireton Road is now Cumberhills Road.

Town Street is now Church Road.

The **dotted blue** line was Battelles Lane and is now Bridle Path No. 13

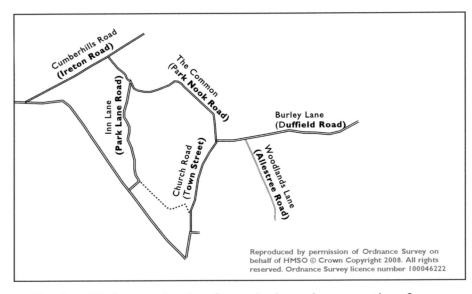

Reproduced by permission of Ordnance Survey on behalf of HMSO © Crown Copyright 2008. All rights reserved. Ordnance Survey licence number 100046222

Matthew Pitt's map showing Quarndon's road names - then & now

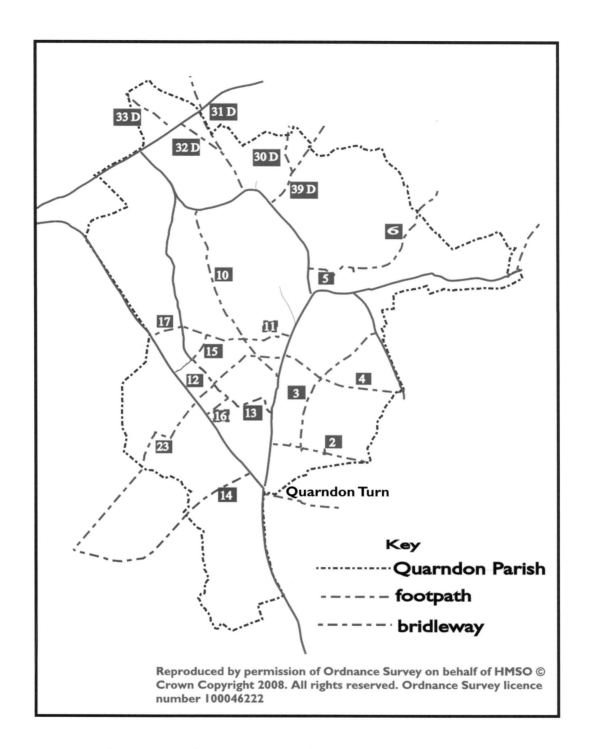

Key

Quarndon Parish
footpath
bridleway

Reproduced by permission of Ordnance Survey on behalf of HMSO ©
Crown Copyright 2008. All rights reserved. Ordnance Survey licence
number 100046222

Quarndon's numbered footpaths & bridleways
Map by Matthew Pitt

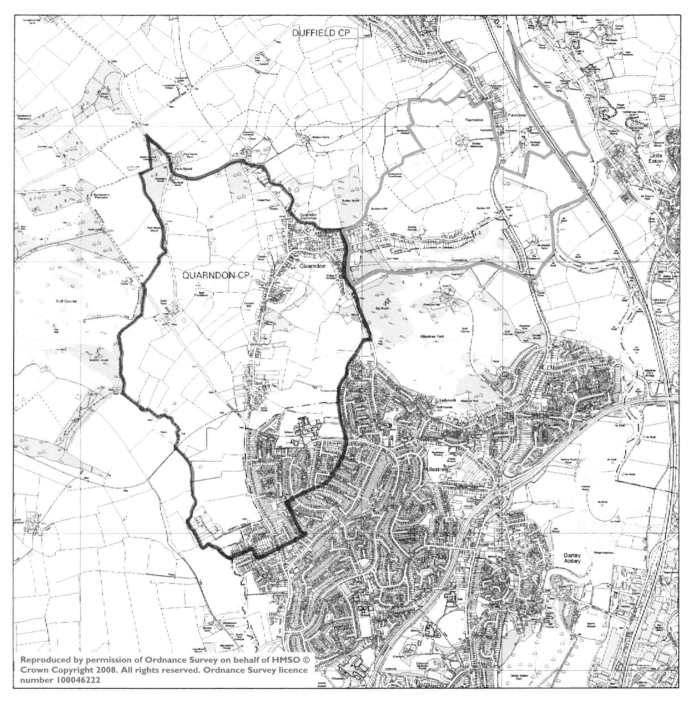

Map of Manors of Quarndon & Burley

By Noel Tornbohm

Quarndon in red; Burley in blue

Reproduced by permission of Ordnance Survey on behalf of HMSO © Crown Copyright 2008. All rights reserved. Ordnance Survey licence number 100046222

8. Farming in Quarndon

By NOEL TORNBOHM, MATTHEW PITT, ROSEMARY LUCAS
& BRYAN HARRIS

FROM time immemorial, all villages had to be self-sufficient. This meant that they needed arable, meadow, pasture and common (or waste) land. Most of the land would be for arable use - ie, the cultivation of cereal crops. Meadows were to produce hay to store for winter feed - animals being turned on to them for pasture once the hay had been gathered. Additional pasture would be found largely on the common land in a village, or on those parts of the arable fields that were left uncultivated from time to time. Those people who were entitled to land were given a share - in the shape of "strips" separated by furrows - of the arable land, each receiving a portion of good, drained and bad, undrained furrow land, together with a changeable share (sometimes through drawing lots) of the meadow. But, although this "ridge & furrow" strip system seemed fair, it had the disadvantage that the strips, being small and far apart, were difficult to develop. Farmers therefore started poaching adjoining strips and enclosing them into the smaller fields.

Evidence of "ridge & furrow" strip system behind the site of Quarndon's former Mill.
(When fields became waterlogged, cattle could 'lie and dry' on the ridges.)

This practice became particularly widespread by the latter half of the 18th century when there was a serious increase in the demand for food. To meet this, landlords, prompted by the desire to increase their rental income, took the opportunity to promote the enclosure of the old open fields. This led to the development of new farming methods, more manageable fields - some of which by now were dedicated to pasture - and the provision of better crops and animals. This also, it has to be said, caused great hardship to many poor people, who lost their right to graze their cattle on the common.

Historically, the village of Quarndon grew from two adjoining manors (see map on *opposite page*). To the north east was the manor of Burley, comprising *Burley Grange*, Burley Wood and both sides of what is now Burley Lane. Originally, this manor had belonged to the monks of Darley Abbey, *Burley Grange* being one of the farms operated by the monks for grazing sheep and cattle and providing cereals and malt for their own use.

To the west and south was the manor of "Quarndon, Quarn, Quorn", etc, which included what is now Montpelier and everything to the west and south of the present Church Road, The Common and Woodlands Lane areas.

Geologically, the southern slope of Quarndon sits uneasily astride the Pendleton Fault - a major fault-line running north-west/south-east across the country, starting beyond Manchester (see *opposite page*, with the pink area to its south west). Immediately north of the line in Quarndon are carboniferous shales, underpinned by limestone, interrupted on the top of the hill by an intrusion of Triassic (or Bunter) sandstones. South of the line is Keuper marl. On and near the sandstone, the soil is a sandy loam, with occasional sandstone outcrops, whilst most of the rest of the village is clay.

As is explained in Chapter 6, in the first half of the eighteenth century, the Curzon family - owners of *Kedleston Hall* and Park (with the head of the family being lord of the manor of Kedleston) - systematically purchased most of Quarndon and much of the surrounding area, including lucrative mining country to the north. They also became lords of the manor of Burley when they purchased the estate from a family called Neville in 1712. The Dukes of Devonshire were lords of the manor of Quarndon from 1764 to 1865.

In 1762, Nathaniel, 1st Baron Scarsdale, commissioned a survey of all the fields, farms and properties in the Quorn part of the village. The following year, a *Terrier* (schedule) listing all the inhabitants and their properties was produced (see frontispiece, *below*). This showed that, by then, most of the land belonged to the Kedleston Estate, but that there existed a surprising number of individual ownerships (freeholds).

Frontispiece: *1763 Terrier*

The Estate owned 430 of the 731 acres (174 out of 296 hectares). There were also freeholds totalling 221 acres (89h). The common land, on which most of the villagers would have the right to graze their stock, and from which they could collect fuel, amounted to 79:32 (acres first: hectares second). As is illustrated by the map on page 38, the site of what is now The Common was indeed common land - funnel-shaped to the south-east so that cattle could be driven home more easily in the evening.

Disregarding smallholdings, there were six farms. These were known later as *The Grange* (46:19), *Bottom* (60: 24), *Springfield* (77:31), *Holly Bank* (136:55), *Bath* (79:32) and *Quarndon Old Hall* (in what is now Old Vicarage Lane, but the *Hall* - see Chapter 1 - was demolished in 1812) (131:53). In those days the farms didn't have names, but were known by the surnames of their tenants (in the same order): William Brookhouse, John Edge, William Sadler, John Sherwin, John Lamb and Joseph Sadler, respectively. Field names as they were in 1839 are shown on page 39.

In the early 19th century the demand for food became even greater when the Napoleonic Wars and bad weather caused a rise in the price of grain. As a result, landowners had considerable incentive to improve the productivity of the land and increase rents. The main impact for Quarndon was on the use of the common land, which was taken away from the villagers - areas to the south of "The Common" being allocated to farms and that on the north to housing plots.

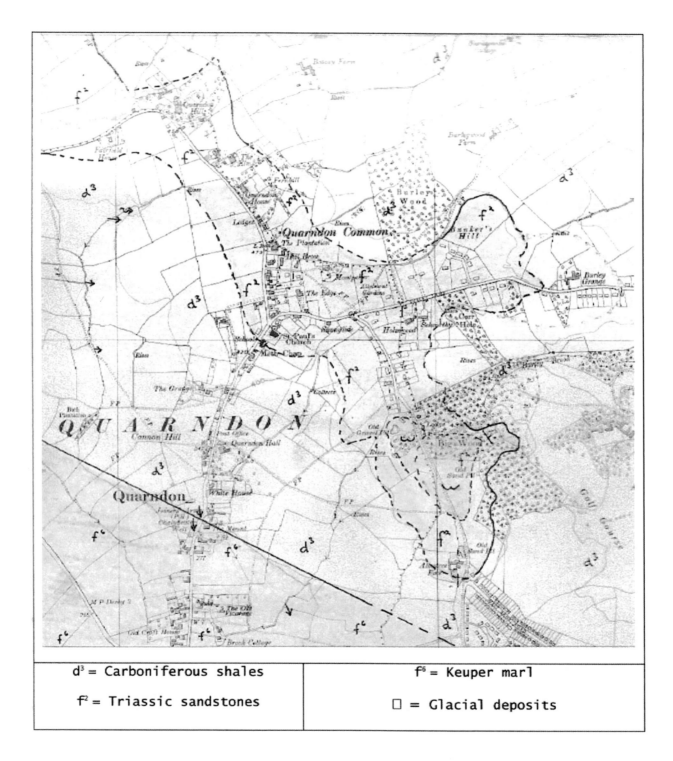

d^3 = Carboniferous shales	f^6 = Keuper marl
f^2 = Triassic sandstones	☐ = Glacial deposits

Geological map of Quarndon

In 1801 the Enclosure Consolidation Act set out the legal steps involved in enclosing land, and, in 1808, a **Commissioner** was appointed to implement the *Quarndon Enclosure Award*. His name was James Dowland and he held his first public meeting at *The Kedleston Inn* (now *The Kedleston Hotel & Restaurant*) on 28th June that year.

As a Commissioner Dowland had huge powers and responsibilities. He needed them to negotiate with the two major landowners of the village, Lord Scarsdale and the Duke of Devonshire - both of whom had been initiators of the Quarndon Enclosure Act. He was required to make a fair division of the land which, in practice, depended on existing ownerships. He organised a detailed survey of the area to assess the values of the different types of land and the rents of any cottages on the land. Wherever possible, parcels of land were grouped together, convenient for access from the farmer's house. Enclosure was also an opportunity for claimants to swap or sell parcels of land (with the agreement of the Commissioner). The other major task was to define new private roads to reach the enclosed land, as well as new or upgraded public roads and footpaths to pass across it.

In the case of Quarndon, much of the land had already been enclosed by private agreement between landowners. Yet the surveying and legal aspects took nine years before Dowland could present his Report on Sunday, 6th April, 1817! This was (and is) a legal document called the **Quarndon Enclosure Award, 1816**.

It was "Inrolled in the Court of our Sovereign Lord the King in the presence of the King himself at Westminster...in the 57th year of the Reign of King George the Third" and includes accurate maps setting out roads and footpaths and the allocation of land. Landowners were required to enclose their fields with quickset (hawthorn) hedges within six months of the publication of the Report - many of those hedges still existing today. In fact, most of the fields created by enclosure can still be identified, either *in situ* or on an Ordnance Survey map at a 1:25000 scale.

Facsimile: Part of the *1816 Quarndon Award*

The enclosure takes in about 100 acres, including common and waste land on Quarndon Common, Esther - or "Easter" - Moor (east of Woodlands Lane), Woodfir Heads (west of Woodlands Lane) and Park Nook (then called Baker's Green). Throughout the document the village is referred to as "Quarn otherwise Quarndon" in the Manor of Little Chester. In the event, no major roads were established, but there was much widening and straightening of existing tracks.

As regards the apportioning of land, Lord Scarsdale received the lion's share at 63.7 acres - much of this land adjoining his existing properties in Kedleston. The Duke of Devonshire received 12.3 acres. Among others to be allocated smaller pieces of land were the Mundy family, Benjamin Smith (of Park Nook) and Robert Battelle.

The sketch map on the *facing page* shows the land apportioned by the *Award*.

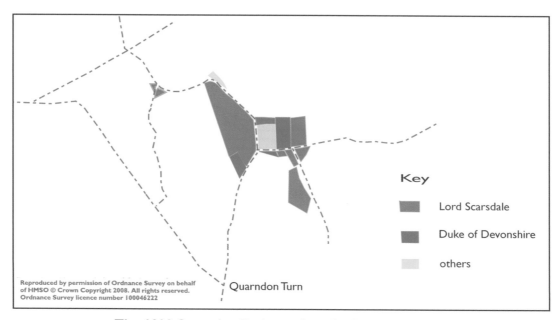

Reproduced by permission of Ordnance Survey on behalf of HMSO © Crown Copyright 2008. All rights reserved. Ordnance Survey licence number 100046222

Quarndon Turn

Key

Lord Scarsdale

Duke of Devonshire

others

The *1816 Quarndon Enclosure Award:* allocation of land
Map by Matthew Pitt

A further survey was carried out for the Curzon family in 1858. By this time, the land comprising The Common had been divided up between the major landlords (following the *1816 Enclosure Award*) in proportion to their existing ownership.

The survey included all their tenants (but didn't extend to those cottages not owned by the estate). For readers whose associations with Quarndon go back several generations, these householders were:

Thomas Ault, William Ault, William Bowler, William Cockayne, Philip Clarke, Joseph Clifford, Marianne Downing, Mrs Draycott, Thomas Fearn, William Ford, Samuel Ford, William Fowke, Joseph Fowkes, William Gallimore, William Norman Gamble, Charles Hampshire, Hannah Hunt, Job Jackson, William Lowe, David Maddocks, R C Matthews, Joseph Sadler, Samuel Sadler, Richard Sherlock, J J Simpson, Miss Sitwell, Charles Slack, Joseph Slack, Sarah Smith, Benjamin Sowter, William Sowter, John Tempest, William Thorpe and Robert Wardle.

The survey also showed that, as a result of the reallocation of the land, coupled with the buying in of most of the freeholds, the Kedleston Estate had increased its ownership to include most of the village (with the exception of those house plots on the former Common, granted by the *1816 Award*).

By now (ie, between 1762 and 1838), the number of farms had increased from six to eleven and the total area of land let by the Kedleston Estate had increased from 430 acres (174h.) to 682 (276h.). Of this, 39% was used for pasture (stock-grazing), 35% for meadow (hay-making) and 26% for the cultivation of crops.

So, although during the 1840s there had been 25 stocking-looms operating in the village (see Chapter 12: *Shops, trades & industries*), until World War 2, Quarndon was mainly an agricultural community, *Bulmer's Directory of 1895* stating: "The soil is a sandy peat and mostly laid down for dairy purposes."

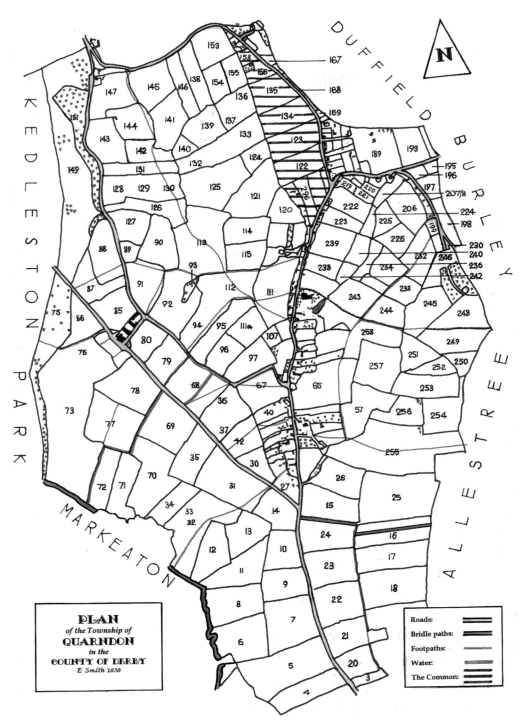

1839 Quarndon Field Map
(Key to field numbers on *facing page*.)

38

Key to field numbers, 1839

(See map on opposite page)

NB 1: In the cross-hatched area at top of map, note the tapering shape of the former Quarndon Common (now The Common), so that, after grazing, the cattle could be funnelled down what is now Church Road. NB 2: Askerfield Avenue (Allestree) is located on the site of Hasker's Fields (16-18).

3 Fitch Pingle, 4 Moseleys, 5 Nether Derby Close, 6 Big Meadow, 7 Cob Thorne, 8 Little Meadow, 9 Cob Thorne, 10 Top Meadow, 11 & 12 Bottom Meadow, 13 Middle Meadow, 14 Top Meadow, 15 Bancroft, 16 Near Hasker, 17 Far Hasker, 18 Hasker, 20 & 21 Top Derby Close, 22 Cob Thorne, 23 Field, 24 Bancroft, 25 Gilgraves, 26 Town End Close, 27 Croft, 30 Leys, 31 Gosslins, 32 & 33 Long Meadow, 34 Little Meadow, 35 Turnpike Close, 36 Pingle, 37 Shear Flatt, 40 Croft, 42 Top Close, 57 Long Orchard, 65 Lower Pasture, 67 Nether Yard, 68 Holding Green, 69 Kedleston Close, 70 Mow Meadow, 71 Little Meadow, 72 Mow Meadow, 73 In Kerry, 76 High Moor Meadow, 77 Nether Moor, 78 High Moor, 79 Holding Green, 80 Grindlestone Close, 85 Home Close, 86 Shoulder of Mutton, 87 Near Oakerleys, 88 Far Oakerleys, 89 Spring Bit, 90 Top Soggs, 91 Bottom Soggs, 92 Bath Close, 93 Bath Plantation, 94 Cannon Hill, 95 Far Cannon Hill, 96 Little Marlpit Close, 97 Big Marlpit Close.

107 Far Close, 111 & 111a Cote Close, 112 Cannon Hill, 113 Dobleys, 114 Far Downsidge, 115 Downsidge, 120 Top Croft, 121 Woodfir, 122 Big Common Close, 123 Common Piece, 124 Little Woodfir, 125 Big Woodfir, 126 Long Pingle, 127 Stony Close, 128 Top Close, 129 Middle Close, 130 Bottom Close, 131 Long Pingle, 132 Bottom Woodfir, 133 Top Woodfir, 134 Common Piece, 135 Common Piece, 136 Dales Woodfir, 137 Marts Woodfir, 138 Long Griff, 139 Big Woodfir, 140 Roundabout, 141 Owlers Close, 142 Little Griff, 143 Granney, 144 Big Griff, 145 Gorsey Griff, 146 Long Griff, 147 Holme Close, 149 Upper Park, 151 Park Nook Wood, 153 Stones Griff, 154 & 155 Part of Griff, 156 Croft, 158 Croft, 167, 168 & 169 Bess o' Barton's Piece, 176 Croft, 189 Common Piece, 193 Allotment to the Poor, 195 Far Field, 196 Croft, 197 Croft, 198 Common Piece, 199 Croft.

206 Hill Close, 207 & 208 Shed Piece, 219 Top Croft, 220 & 221 Bottom Croft, 222 & 223 Nook Close, 224 Hunger Hill, 225 & 226 Oak Tree Close, 230 Three cornered Piece, 232 Hill Ways, 233 Far Hillways, 234 Great Hillways, 236 Bog Piece, 238 & 239 Barn Close, 240 Bottom Carr, 242 Little Barn Close, 243 Hillways, 244 Far Hillways, 245, 245a, 248 & 249 Easter Moor, 246 Far End of Easter Moor, 250 Old Sam Smith's Bit, 251 Frost's Close, 252 Frost's Little Close, 253 Buxton's Close, 254 Middle Plank Field, 255 Plank Field, 256 Middle Plank Field, 257 Owler Bars, 258 Top Pasture, 296a Common Piece.

Farms & Farmhouses: Then & Now

Today there are still those in the village who can remember a dozen or so working farms in what is now Quarndon. Coming up the village from the south, (passing the site of *Bottom* and *Springfield Farms*, past *Holly Bank Farm*) to as far as *Burley Grange*, then cutting back through Montpelier to travel down The Common to *Mulberry House* and up The Common (taking in *Botany* and the former *Quarndon Hill Farms*) to *Park Nook Farm*, then up to *Champion Farm* (where some of the fields are in Quarndon) and the former *Cumberhills Farm* and back, then down Inn Lane to *The Kedleston Hotel* (*Bath Farm*), the farmhouses were, or are, located as follows:

Bottom Farm Cottages   The site today

These stood just north of the present No. 1 Church Road. (See account by Fred Kelsey on page 45.) Frank Stone remembers gathering watercress and catching sticklebacks in the stream running through the farm.

Springfield Farm: the house   *Springfield Farm*: outbuildings

Now a private house: 31 Church Road. To the *left* of the house were the farmyard and cowsheds. To the *right* are some original farm buildings, now converted for domestic use. (See *Quarndon Bricks*, page 78.)

Holly Bank Farm: **the extended house**

Holly Bank Farm: **outbuildings**

The farmhouse has been extended for private use. The buildings around the farmyard are awaiting residential development. In 1923, all the cattle here were destroyed as a result of a Foot & Mouth epidemic.

Fields Farm

The site today

Off Church Road, behind the Senior Citizens' Bungalows. Now re-built on the same site as a private house.

Burley Grange Farm

The site today

This was demolished in 2001 (see page 48) and replaced by a private house: *Burley Grange*. The latter won the 2003 Federation of Plastering & Drywall Contractors' Regional Award and the 2004 *Daily Telegraph* "Best Luxury House" Gold Award.

Montpelier Farm

The site today

Demolished. Site now occupied by a private house: No. 12 Montpelier.

(There was also a farm at what is now *Mulberry House*, 6 The Common, formerly the Post Office - see Chapter 12: *Shops, trades & industries*. It is said that Fred Wright, the farmer, turned out his cattle to do what they'd got to do on the road so they didn't mess up his farmyard!)

Botany Farm: the farmhouse today

Botany Farm: cattle grazing

This farm, off The Common, in the most northerly part of the village, is the only dairy farm left in Quarndon, with a herd of 90 Friesian cows on 150 acres. Arable land is also rented in Duffield parish.

Quarndon Hill Farm

This was established by Hadden and Mary Richardson in 1947 with two Jersey cows. The herd has since been sold. (See James Richardson's account on page 49.)

Park Nook Farm: the farmhouse today

Park Nook Farm: sheep & cattle grazing

Bought at auction, 25th March, 1825, by the Curzon family. Still a working farm.

Photo: David Widdows

Champion Farm

Still a working farm on the Kedleston Estate, with part of the land in Quarndon.

Cumberhills Farm

Bath Farm

Now *Cumberhills Cottage*. No longer a farm.

(See Chapter 11: *The Kedleston Hotel*)

Life on the farm

Spanning a period from the late 19th century to the end of the 20th century, here are five personal accounts of life on four local farms.

(a) *Springfield Farm*

An undated cutting (certainly post-1895) from *The Cable* newspaper carries an interview with Samuel Osborne - "a leading dairy farmer in Derbyshire" - who was the tenant of *Springfield Farm* (31 Church Road) - "a very prettily-situated holding....and may be recognised by the stone gate-posts, which are characteristic of most of the farms on the [Kedleston] estate".

Stone gatepost & wall, *Springfield Farm*

Photo: David Widdows

In the interview, Osborne explains that his 250 acres represented three farms thrown into one.

"The arrangement," he complains, "is inconvenient because more men are wanted for the dispatch of business than if I had one large block of buildings. There is a lot of extra work, such as candle-lighting for milking."

His labour force, he explains, consisted of "three men at £1 per week and perquisites, such as coal all year round; three who receive £40 a year, with board and lodging; and an Irishman, who earns £12 as harvest wages".

He adds: "Most of the men have been working for me for more than twenty years. I have never had any difficulty with them."

He went on to say that there were fifty cows on the farm, five horses and forty hens. He also ran a flourishing retail shop in Green Lane, Derby. Asked if he had time for any public work, he replied: "I am a member of the Derbyshire County Council, of the Belper District Council and of the Parish Council in Quarndon. I was also secretary to the Derbyshire Dairy Farmers' Association for thirteen years, retiring at Christmas, 1895".

(b) *Bottom Farm*

In the 1980s, **Fred Kelsey** wrote:

"My association with Quarndon began on 19th December, 1925, when my family took up residence at *Old Croft Cottage,* which stood in the stack-yard of *Bottom Farm* (on the west side of Church Road, just north of Quarndon Turn). It had two very low rooms downstairs and two rooms upstairs, which were very lofty and cold. Stuck on the end of the house was a wash house in which was the only water tap, an old gas stove and a big copper.

Drawing of *Bottom Farm & Old Croft Cottage* by George Kelsey (brother of Fred)

When we first went there, the floor of the wash house was of old bricks - very worn and uneven - but, after a few years, these were replaced by concrete. Also downstairs was a pantry - almost pitch dark on account of a very small window.

The front door opened right into the living room, in which was an old grate consisting of a fire, an oven on one side and a cracked boiler on the other. There was no electricity or hot water system. We were lit by gas when we could afford it and every drop of hot water had to be heated on the fire. Toilet facilities consisted of a bucket in a hut up the back yard.

We weren't very well off, but living on the farm gave us some perks, which helped us to survive the Depression of the 1920s and 1930s. Economies in heating and lighting were necessary: the cottage was lit by gas, but we took candles to bed and heating was helped by using local timber.

In about 1936, the labour situation on the farm got desperate and I assisted at the farm before going off to school. I would then leave home at 8, walk over Burley Hill to Duffield Road and there catch a bus to Herbert Strutt's School in Belper."

Sheep-shearing at *Bottom Farm*. Left to right: Beryl Kelsey (later Frost); Eric Broadhead (killed in operations over Germany, 23/24.5.42. See page 173); George Kelsey, Snr.

45

(c) *Burley Grange Farm*

Burley Grange Farm

Burley Grange - originally a working farm for Darley Abbey - included a monastic barn in which wool, grain, hay and timber (from Duffield Forest) were stored. It was demolished in 2001.

Maurice Oakley, who was born at *Burley Grange*, writes:

"My father, George - Brailsford & District Ploughing & Hedgecutting Society Champion Ploughman, 1908 - ran *Burley Grange Farm* for a number of years. I used to deliver milk across the fields in all weathers. (They were building Allestree Golf Course at the time.) When my father died, my mother (Alice Mary, known as 'May') ran the farm for seven years.

There was no electricity, no gas, one spring supplying the whole farm and a copper in the kitchen, where she washed everything. I don't know how she managed it all! Our source of income was from the milk we produced. Most of the food we ate we'd grown ourselves."

Roof beams in a *Burley Grange* barn

Photos: Mattew Pitt

Aerial view of *Burley Grange Farm*

Source unknown

Harold Coulthread, who retired in 1990 as tenant manager of the farm, writes:

"I first came to Quarndon in 1950 as a farm worker at *Burley Grange,* where my father was farm manager for Mr Alfred Bowmer. We had a pedigree herd of Friesian cattle, with 28 dairy cows. Milking was done by a vacuum pipe into buckets, then cooled and run into churns, which were collected every day. There was also a bull-pen. Eggs from 3,000 deep-litter hens were sold to the Co-operative Society and a few pigs were kept for our own consumption - any surplus going to local butchers. As there were only 45 acres of land attached to the farm, we rented 100 acres of adjoining land for hay and silage - mostly in Allestree Park. Apart from my father and me, the only other help we had was seasonal and temporary.

In 1955, having married a local girl, I moved to *Quarndon Hill* as farm manager for the Richardson family. Here was a well-established Jersey herd which had won prizes at shows throughout the country. The milk was of very high butter fat content and the cream was separated and sold locally and in Derby.

After my father retired in 1970, I was offered the tenancy of *Burley Grange* at a rent of £1,170 per annum. This imposing brick-built 3-storey farmhouse, with its traditional barns and outbuildings dating from about 1750, enjoyed

47

spectacular views over the Derwent valley and was a very pleasant spot at which to live and work. It also had the advantage of a water supply from a well behind the house.

Returning with my wife and two children, I started a Friesian pedigree attested herd. This meant only buying in cattle from accredited, brucellosis-free and enzootic bovine leucosis-tested herds. The buildings had to be thoroughly cleaned, disinfected and quarantined for six weeks before being passed by the Ministry of Agriculture. Labouring for a builder helped to finance the venture and eventually the herd was built up sufficiently to warrant the purchase of a milking parlour and bulk tank.

Quarn Galore Craig

Source unknown

Averaging a yield of 200 gallons of milk a day, I obtained a retail licence to sell milk at the farm. I also bought a separator to enable me to sell cream and feed the skimmed milk to the pigs. I sold several bulls to the Milk Marketing Board and *Quarn Galore Craig* (pictured *above right*) was a proven sire who was widely used for artificial insemination purposes throughout the United Kingdom.

I worked the farm with the assistance of an agricultural student, my wife helping with the dairy work and bookkeeping. But in 1990, after 46 years of farming, and with rented ground at over £50 per acre, a dispersal sale of cattle was held and corn was grown on the original 45 acres. In 2001, farming on the site ceased completely when *Burley Grange* was sold and demolished and a private house was built on the site."

Photo: Derby Evening Telegraph

"Harold, a popular baritone with the Belper Musical Theatre, always claimed that excerpts from musicals relaxed his Friesian herd. Here they're treated to a final rendering before he sold up and retired." (*Derby Evening Telegraph*)

THE
QUARN DISPERSAL SALE
OF
PEDIGREE, EBL ATTESTED, LEPTOSPIROSIS VACCINATED
FRIESIAN CATTLE

QUARN CRAIG TWINKLE RM(5), RMX, RML, (VG-84), lot 4

Thursday September 13, 1990
(12 noon)
———
H. D. & S. M. COULTHREAD
BURLEY GRANGE FARM
QUARNDON
DERBY

Sale catalogue

(d) *Quarndon Hill Farm*

James Richardson recalls:

"In 1947, food was very scarce and my parents decided to farm the land at *Quarndon Hill*. The fields had been neglected and the soil was poor. They had an existing cow shed with accommodation for four cows, so two pedigree Jersey cows - Jessie and Flower - and a few pigs were purchased, along with a huge hay barn and a brand new Ferguson tractor and plough. I was taught to drive this at the age of 10!

We employed a herdsman, but, though we were well served with fresh milk, cream, butter, eggs and bacon, it was soon realised that there was not enough work for one man, so the herd was eventually expanded to 36. *Quarndon Hill* was then worked as a mixed farm and I remember harvesting the corn, which was great fun. The binder would cut the corn and we would follow behind stooking the sheaves. Later, a great traction engine would arrive with a threshing machine, driven by an enormous leather belt. I used to bag up the grain and the straw was baled and stored in the hay barn.

When my father died in 1968, running a dairy farm proved too onerous for my mother, so the Jersey herd was sold. She then bought a Charolais (beef) herd, but they proved very expensive and brought their problems, so they were eventually sold. The farm ceased to operate in 1979."

Life on the land: Then & Now

Photo: Derby Evening Telegraph

In the early 1940s

Park Nook Farm: **Working the land, 1986**

Park Nook Farm: **Combine harvester, 1986**

Park Nook Farm: **2005**

Courtesy: Rod Jewell Collection

Photo: Liz Harris

The Joiners' Arms

Above: Before it was rendered, painted white and extended. Note also the positioning of the door, steps and garden steps in the Church Road wall.
Below: The Joiners' today

9. Quarndon's pubs

OF Quarndon's five original public houses - or rather, the ones that we know about - only *The Joiners' Arms* survives. (*The Kedleston Hotel & Restaurant* is featured separately in Chapter 11.)

The name *Joiners' Arms* - Quarndon's longest-serving public house - clearly originates from the period 1759 to 1765 - its heyday - when it was frequented by the joiners and other craftsmen building *Kedleston Hall*. The original building, which was part of the Kedleston Estate, dates from the 17th century. The front of the building (facing Church Road) is mid-18th century. It originally (see *opposite page*) had steps leading up to a doorway and a gate from the street.

Ale has been served from these premises from as early as the 17th century. From the records of the Derbyshire Quarter Sessions we know that, in 1769, Matthew Hampshire was licensed as a victualler. The pub was granted a full licence in 1869.

One of Matthew's descendants was Ellen Hampshire, whose *History of Quarndon* is frequently referred to in this book. She was born at *The Joiners'* in 1870 - the last of a family of nine - and died, aged 102, in 1972. In her book, written in the early 1930s, she wrote that her family had managed the ale-house in an unbroken line for 300 years.

Over that time the popularity of Quarndon as a spa village (see Chapter 10) clearly boosted a trade in refreshment, accommodation and stabling - the Hampshires being well equipped to cater for all these requirements and much more besides.

The *Joiners' Arms* from the south - before and after white rendering

Photo: Derek Wigley

As is explained in Chapter 12, in their workshops behind the Chalybeate Well, the Hampshires employed wheelwrights, joiners (Ellen Hampshire's grandfather had played a prominent part in the building of *Kedleston Hall*), undertakers, builders and painters and decorators. In Bulmer's *1895 Directory*, Charles & George Hampshire are described as "Victuallers and brewers, joiners, builders, wheelwrights and blacksmiths". By 1900, "large and small parties" could be accommodated, and, in 1925, the Misses Catherine and Elizabeth Hampshire advertised that, as well as providing "blacksmiths, joiners and wheelwrights" they catered for "cyclists and parties".

On 3rd October, 1866, the Smoke Room of *The Joiners'* was the first building in the village to be lit by gas. This was supplied from a gas works in Duffield, which had been built by a member of the Hampshire family. In Ellen Hampshire's words: "The village was illuminated with stars and crowns in various parts to celebrate the event".

Lot No. 130, *The Joiners' Arms*, of the 1931 "Great Sale" inventory reads: "Tap room, smoke room, parlour, serving bar, 4 cellars, sitting room, kitchen, pantry, passage, brewhouse, spirit room, 4 bedrooms, maids' room, bathroom, WC, attic, 2 staircases. Outbuildings: coalhouse & dairy, ash place and earth closet, 2 pig styes, oil store & paint shed, loft over, loose box, WC, urinal, cowshed with byng, stable for 2, fodder store, mixing place & corn store with grain pit, blacksmith's shop with large joiner's workshop & store over."

According to Frank Stone: "In the early 1930s, *The Joiners' Arms* only had a 6-day licence, so, on Sundays, the regular drinkers would walk to *The White Hart* in Duffield and return over Bunkers Hill."

This links with an account given by Enid Knight, great-niece of Ellen Hampshire:

"As children in the 1920s, we were only allowed to visit *The Joiners'* on Sundays. This was because the Hampshire family didn't want to expose us to the spectacle of men drinking beer. But when we were there one Sunday I noticed spittoons on the floor and asked Aunt Nellie what they were for. She was too embarrassed to admit that the men spat in them, so she said instead: 'They're for cats to use if they need the toilet!'"

In 1978 the front and south walls of the building were rendered and painted white. In 1996, a red brick extension, housing a Function Room, was added to the north of the building. In the year 2000 *East Midlands In Bloom* Competition *The Joiners'* received the Judges' Award for its floral displays.

Ellen Hampshire

***The Joiners'* in bloom**

The other Quarndon pubs were **The Tiger**, originally called **The Salt Box** (on the site of the former residential home, *The Edge*), **The Pig & Whistle**, **The King's Head** (see Chapter 16: *The Quandary*) and **The William IV**.

Our pictures show two of these former watering-holes.

The Pig & Whistle (now demolished) stood on Burley Lane and straddled the pre-1984 boundary.

The former **William IV** pub (No 93-95 *Hall Cottages*, Church Road) is an 18th century Grade II-listed red brick, three-storey building - once three separate houses - with a 19th century brick porch and one-storey wing. John Farnsworth, the present owner-occupier, believes that, during Quarndon's heyday as a spa village, the *William IV* may have been a house of ill repute! It may even have provided the "wretched lodging and entertainment" that Daniel Defoe referred to when reporting on his visit to Quarndon in 1727. (See Chapter 10). In the mid- to late 19th century, it's believed that the property was bought - and closed down as a public house - by a disapproving member of the Sitwell family living opposite at *Quarndon Hall*. (According to Frank Stone, the building was a boys' boarding school for a time, with the dormitory on the top floor.)

The Pig & Whistle (Demolished)

Photo: David Widdows

The former *William IV* pub.

10. The Chalybeate

*(The Editor wishes to thank **CHRISTINE LEATHLEY** of Duffield - a retired pharmacist - for explaining [in square brackets] some of the scientific terms.)*

*Cartoon illustrations by **PAMELA COPESTAKE**.*

The Chalybeate Spring

TODAY it's difficult to imagine that Quarndon was once a celebrated spa village - "the Malvern of Derbyshire" - when visitors flocked to its Chalybeate Well (technically "Spring") to take the waters. This Grade II-listed crenulated structure, with its three pointed arches, is situated just south of *The Joiners' Arms* on Church Road.

The word Chalybeate (officially pronounced "ka-lib-e-at", but known locally as The "Challybeet") comes from the Latin *chalybeatus*, meaning "containing or tasting of iron".

Commemorative plaque

Photo: Don Hall

Daniel Defoe

© National Portrat Gallery, London

Photo: David Widdows

Lion's head pourer

Various 17th, 18th and 19th century writers have referred to the healing qualities of the water that once flowed from the lion's head pourer in the nearside bottom left hand corner of the Spring.

A plaque on the back wall of the Spring commemorates a visit in 1727 by Daniel Defoe (author of *Robinson Crusoe*), after which he wrote in his *Tour Through the Whole Island of Great Britain*: "We came to Quarn or Quarden, a little ragged but noted village, where there is a famous chalybeate spring, to which abundance of people go in the season to drink the water, as also a cold bath. We found the wells, as custom bids us call them, pretty full of company, the waters good, and very physical, but wretched lodging and entertainment."

Defoe may well have been versed in the works of earlier commentators on the Spring.

In 1663 Phillip Kinder, in his *Historie of Darbyshire*, had written that Quarndon's well water was "good against vomiting, comforts ye stomach, cures ye ulcers of ye bladder, stopps all fluxes [abnormal discharge of blood or excrement from the body], helps conception, stays bleeding in ye breast and at ye srige." The iron content, he continued, was "good for ye Splen and Urines, is good against ye Colick, and ache in Joynts, cures tertian and quartan feavers [fevers occurring every third or fourth day] and ye stone [a hard secretion in the body - especially in the kidney or gall bladder - formed by minerals]."

William Woolley, in his *History of Derbyshire* (1712), wrote of Quarndon: "It has a chalybeate spring, which is pretty much resorted to in the summer."

Other writers commended the waters for their "Specific in Coughs, Asthma, Consumption, Spitting of blood, Hyppa, Cachexy [a condition of weakness of body, precipitated by chronic disease], Chlorosis [a severe form of anaemia due to iron deficiency - especially in young women] and for their particular serviceability in all cases of debility from free living or debauchery". (Presumably, a cure for hangovers!)

Dr Paul Hodson, of Burley Lane, writes:

"Malaria was endemic in England from the 16th to the 19th centuries - mainly in the marshes of the south and east, from Southampton to the Wash, but also in some areas of the north and west. Infection was with two or four strains of the malaria parasite - namely *Plasmodium vivax* and *Plasmodium malariae*.

These two varieties are not usually fatal, but cause fever, which spikes every 48 hours with *vivax* - hence *tertian fever* - and every 72 hours with *malariae* - hence *quartan fever*. The *tertian* and *quartan* agues were mentioned by Shakespeare a number of times and by Chaucer in *The Priest's Tale*.

Oliver Cromwell is probably the best known person to have suffered from *quartan fever*.

Sunday afternoon sermons

Flux refers to a pathological discharge of fluid from the body - eg, blood, mucous or pus. The reference to *flux* almost certainly refers to dysentery, which was a severe, dangerous and not uncommon disorder - described by Hippocrates among others. The disease is characterised by the sudden onset of abdominal cramps, bloating and severe diarrhoea - often with blood and mucous. It was frequently fatal - sometimes after a protracted, painful and debilitating illness.

Henry V died of the *'bloody flux'* in 1422 and Sir Francis Drake in 1596."

As for the Chalybeate structure, during the Commonwealth (1649-60), Sunday afternoon sermons (often lasting two or three hours!) were preached "for the benefit of visitors" from the battlements by the Rev'd Joseph Swetnam, the Puritan Vicar of All Saints' Church, Derby (now Derby Cathedral).

Later, during the reign of William & Mary, the Bishop of Lichfield reported that "the Spaw" [Spa] "was frequented, but the services in the Church were of a very desultory character".

In 1802, George Lipscombe wrote: "Quarndon water is turned to a very deep purple, with infusion of galls [may be an abnormal swelling of plant tissue caused by insects or micro-organisms, or bile - black or yellow - secreted by the liver]. At the bottom of the glass a dark green colour is produced. It soon loses its carbonic acid gas on being exposed to the common atmosphere and the iron which had been held in solution by that acid is then precipitated." [Iron in the water will be kept in solution by the weak carbonic acid. When the acidity changes - either by exposure to the atmosphere or by the addition of an alkali - the chemical compound formed will appear as solid particles in suspension, which may settle down.]

Marjorie Sulley & Reg Wibberley, in their book, *Historical Vignettes of Quarndon*, relate that "in the early part of the 20th century, when Bunkers Hill was a favourite spot for outings from Derby, many people stopped at the Well to fill jugs and jars from the slow trickle of water. Also, the schoolmaster, Mr Rylatt, would send a pupil daily with a jam-jar during the morning break to collect the water - the jar later being collected". Frank Stone recalls: "As children, we used to fill jars from the lion's head and sell the contents for sixpence!" Ellen Hampshire noted that "If an oak chip is placed in the water, or if it is used for making tea, it turns black".

Topping up the bottle

In 1953, Henry Miller, a 71-year-old Quarndon resident, told a *Derby Evening Telegraph* reporter about a friend of his "in private service at one of the larger houses in the neighbourhood" who was sent by his master to buy a bottle of whisky. "As he was returning home he succumbed to the temptation of opening the bottle and taking a nip to help him on his way...He then topped up the bottle at the Well. Those who enjoy a moral tale will be pleased to hear that the whisky turned black and the fraud was discovered!"

As for the actual date and architect of Quarndon's present "Gothic" structure - which once was roofed and included an attendant's room (behind the door on the left) and a bath - the year 1760 has been suggested.

Maxwell Craven believes that it might have been designed by the Derby architect, Joseph Pickford, 1736-82, "then clerk of works at Kedleston, whose younger son was for many years perpetual curate of Quarndon & Little Eaton".

The same year, a *Sulphur Bath House* - part of which remains today, surrounded by Kedleston Park Golf Club - was built in the grounds of *Kedleston Hall* (see *below*). The water temperature was 53 degrees Fahrenheit (11.66 Celsius), while at Quarndon it was 49F (9.44C). Buxton and Matlock could boast 82F (27.77C), but before the development of both spa towns - and of the rail and improved road links to them - they hardly posed any competition. At the height of its popularity, water from Quarndon and Kedleston was sold in Derby Market Place at a penny a quart.

Photo: Don Hall
Curzon Papers, Kedleston Hall

The *Sulphur Bath House* in Kedleston Park

Courtesy: Derby Local Studies Library

Selling water in Derby Market Place

61

So why does medicinal water no longer flow from the lion's head pourer in Quarndon? The answer lies in a series of earth tremors over a 40-year period. The first is said to have occurred around 1863. Even so, in 1895, the Parish Council was noting that "the Spa Well is of very great advantage to the village" and that "the tank should be flushed every week".

Two years later, another tremor occurred, then a third on 24th March, 1903, which reduced it to a trickle. It's thought that the earth tremor felt across the Midlands in 1956 may have stemmed the flow entirely. Also (see Chapter 8) Noel Tornbohm believes that, as a result of the earth tremors, one side of the Pendleton Fault slipped relative to the other and so cut off the Spring.

In 1943 the Chalybeate (originally owned by the Curzon family) was presented to the Parish Council by Offiler's Brewery. In 1955 a butcher's mobile shop collided with a pillar supporting the central arch (see *below*), costing £130 in repairs. The following year another £129 was spent on restoration work. In 1972 £513 worth of damage was caused by a car.

Meanwhile, in 1967, the Ministry of Housing & Local Government announced that the Well had been included in the List of Buildings of Special Architectural & Historic Interest.

Photo: *Derby Evening Telegraph*

The Chalybeate, after the 1955 collision

Photos: David Widdows

Quarndon's Millennium Well Dressing

Lee Martin & Michael Crawley

In the year 2000, as part of Quarndon's Millennium Celebrations, the Chalybeate was the venue for the village's first Well Dressing.

It was put together by a team led by **Lee Martin** of *The Joiners' Arms* from a design by the local artist, **Michael Crawley**.

The theme - an allusion to the impeded flow of the spring! - was the familiar passage from *Psalm 23:* **"He leads me beside still waters."**

Courtesy: Curzon Papers, Kedleston Hall

The Kedleston Hotel
Top: **An early 19th century engraving. (Note the stables, now demolished, at the back.)**
Bottom: **The *Hotel* today.**

11. *The Kedleston Hotel*

By DON HALL & BRYAN HARRIS

WHILE Robert Adam was building the new *Kedleston Hall* (taking over from the architects, Matthew Brettingham and James Paine), he is also believed to have designed and supervised the building of the three-storey, Grade II*-listed, redbrick *New Inn* - a "posting house and coaching inn", now known as *The Kedleston Hotel & Restaurant*.

From an advertisement in the *Derby Mercury* of 20th February, 1758, we know that an establishment existed "near the SPAW" [spa], known as "*The Kedleston Inn*", serving the "Neatest Wines" and providing "Best Accommodation of all Sorts".

As is explained in Chapter 7, in 1760, Sir Nathaniel Curzon gained permission to relocate the turnpike which had passed along the front of the old *Kedleston Hall*. In preparation for this it would appear that, early in the previous year, he had had the *Inn* demolished. However, an advertisement in the *Mercury* of 24th May, 1759, suggests that some temporary measures must have been put in place:

> "WHEREAS it has been reported, that the INN at KEDLESTON was taken down, and [that there is] no Reception for the GENTLEMEN and LADIES that uses the BATHS, *this is to inform the PUBLIC,*
>
> That there are erected Two Private BATHS, with Dwelling Rooms adjoining; and that the said INN is kept as usual, with the best Accommodation for GENTLEMEN and LADIES,
>
> By your most obedient Servant, JOHN LAMB"

What we do know from records is that in June, 1760, Samuel Wyatt, Robert Adam's Clerk of Works, moved bricks, stone and sawn timber to a site on the north east side of the new turnpike - the former riding avenue known as "All Saints' Walk" - and that the building of the *New Inn* (later re-using the old name, *The Kedleston Inn*) began that year, as part of *Bath Farm*.

The front - flanked by one-storey wings - has a Doric column on either side of 20th century windows and a glass door. According to Nikolaus Pevsner (*The Buildings of England: Derbyshire*, publ. Penguin Books), this was originally a *porte-cochère* - a porch large enough to admit wheeled vehicles. So, today, we must imagine an original throughway, front-to-rear, similar to that at the *Red Lion Hotel* in Wirksworth.

The Red Lion Hotel, **Wirksworth**

The north-east (rear) side of the hotel has a 20th century glazed area between two protruding wings. Five metres inside are two large pillars. These once formed the exit to the courtyard and stabling area - now the hotel car park.

One of the purposes of the *Inn* was to accommodate visitors to the Sulphur Baths in Kedleston Park and to serve "health tourists" of the day who came to take the waters of Quarndon's Chalybeate Well (see Chapter 10). Among the distinguished guests of the *New Inn* were Admiral George Rodney (who, in 1759, had bombarded the port of Le Havre and destroyed the French flotilla about to invade England) and the lexicographer, critic and poet, Dr Samuel Johnson.

Kedleston Hotel, **rear entrance**

Photo: Don Hall

Sir Nathaniel, who was created First Baron Scarsdale in 1761, appointed as the first manager of the *New Inn* his former butler, John Lamb (see *previous page*) and instructed his builders to design an archery range and bowling green and lay a path to the *Sulphur Springs* and *Bath House* in Kedleston Park.

© National Maritime Museum, Greenwich, London

Admiral Rodney

© Tate, London 2008

Dr Johnson by Sir Joshua Reynolds

In 1859 Robert Goodson, the then proprietor, was advertising locally that he would be "happy to accommodate Pleasure Parties and Private Families on the most reasonable terms, who can rely upon the Choicest Wines and Spirits Imported". "Mineral bathing" was "open daily" and "excellent stabling" was on offer. But, by 1866, such was the rival popularity of Buxton, Harrogate, Matlock and the Midland spa towns that the demand for an inn declined and the building was let by the Kedleston Estate as a farmhouse. In 1868, gas was installed at a cost of £52.

Photo: Frederick J Boyes

The Hunt meets at *The Kedleston Hotel*, 1916

From 1874 to 1887 the farm was leased by Edward Kidger, who is listed in the 1881 Quarndon Census as a "farmer of 248 acres, employing five labourers". In November, 1887, the annual rent to the Kedleston Estate was £223 2s. In the Foot & Mouth epidemic of 1923, 113 stock were destroyed.

Courtesy: Kedleston Estate

***Bath Farm* Barn**

Among the adjacent farm buildings today is a Grade II-listed, red brick, late 18th century **Barn**. The walls are punctuated with three rows of breather openings on either side of a 20th century sliding door.

In the 1960s the tenant farmer was Frank Morley, who had been born there. According to the late Ivan Cope, who lived at 115 Church Road: "One morning, my border collie went missing. Eventually I found him penning sheep into a corner. They belonged to Frank Morley, who ran *Bath Farm*. When I rang Frank to apologise he offered to buy my totally untrained dog! But I wouldn't part with him. On another occasion, the dog was spotted penning imaginary sheep!"

Photo: David Widdows

Bath Farm

According to the late Ursula Eddowes:"I went to lots of parties at *Bath Farm*. A lovely farm and the Morleys were a lovely family - all nine of them."

Eventually the Morleys found the building to be too large and, with dry rot on the upper floors, it was in urgent need of costly repair and modernisation, so the 2nd Viscount Scarsdale built them a house opposite. (The garden now incorporates the original *New Inn* bowling green).

After several years the property was leased to David Cox, a local businessman, who reopened it as a 17-bedroom hotel on 19th November, 1970. At the time of publication the hotel has 12 bedrooms and *Bath Farm* is used to grow wheat and maize and to rear replacement dairy heifers for *Inn Farm*, Weston Underwood.

Opposite the North Gate to Kedleston Park and situated close to the Quarndon parish boundary is a Grade II-listed wrought iron **Screen** (see *opposite page*), built in 1767 by Benjamin Yates. It is part of the original screen which once stood at the north front of *Kedleston Hall*. It was moved to its present position in 1916.

Additional information: Peakdale Research

Photo: David Widdows

Bath Farm buildings, Inn Lane

Wrought iron screen

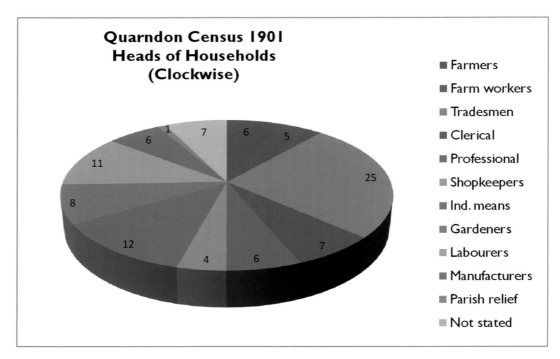

**Quarndon Census 1901
Heads of Households
(Clockwise)**

- Farmers
- Farm workers
- Tradesmen
- Clerical
- Professional
- Shopkeepers
- Ind. means
- Gardeners
- Labourers
- Manufacturers
- Parish relief
- Not stated

6, 5, 25, 7, 6, 4, 12, 8, 11, 6, 1, 7

Pie-charts: Matthew Pitt

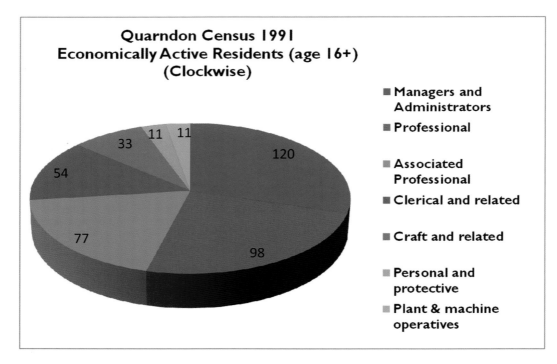

**Quarndon Census 1991
Economically Active Residents (age 16+)
(Clockwise)**

- Managers and Administrators
- Professional
- Associated Professional
- Clerical and related
- Craft and related
- Personal and protective
- Plant & machine operatives

120, 98, 77, 54, 33, 11, 11

1901 & 1991 Census pie-charts

12. Shops, trades & industries

The undermentioned Houses are situate within the boundaries of the ... Page 9

HOUSES	Name and Surname of each Person	RELATION to Head of Family	Condition as to Marriage	Age last Birthday of Males / Females	PROFESSION OR OCCUPATION	Employer, Worker, or Own account	If Working at Home	WHERE BORN	(1) Deaf and Dumb (2) Blind (3) Lunatic (4) Imbecile, feeble-minded
	George Booth	head	M	74	Grocer & Shopkeeper	worker	at home	Cheshire Macclesfield	/
	Mary Do	wife	M	72				Derbys: Ashbourne	
	John Holbrooke	head	M	53	Garden Labourer	worker		" Shottle	
	Harriet Do	wife	M	53				Quarndon	
	Letty Do	daur	S	23					
	Robert Rylatt	head	M	41	Certificated Schoolmaster			Lincs Boston	/
	Eliza Do	wife	M	40				Derbys: Derby	
	Mary A. Do	sister	S	33	/			Lincs: Boston	/
	William Frarn	head	M	36	Agricultural Labourer	worker		Derbys: C. Broughton	
	Eliza Do	wife	M	36	/			" Hilton	
	Ernest W. Do	son		12	/			" Allestree	
	Albert Do	son		7	/			"	
	Emily M. Do	daur		2	/			" Quarndon	
	James Hall	head	M	31	Gas Yard Labourer	worker		" Holland	
	Mary Do	wife	M	40	/			" Oakerthorpe	

Facsimile of page from 1901 Census

SINCE the first Census of 1841, much information has been documented regarding Quarndon's fluctuating population and the changes in its trade, industry and employment patterns.

In 1901, of the 98 heads of households recorded, 25 were trades-people, 12 were of independent means, 11 were labourers, 8 were gardeners, 7 were clerks, 7 were labelled as "occupation not given", 6 were professional, 6 were manufacturers, 6 were farmers, 5 were farm workers, 4 were shopkeepers and one was on parish relief.

Between 1801 and 1841, the population of Quarndon rose from 357 to 556.

Between 1851 and 1861, it dropped from 529 to 496 and the number of houses unoccupied rose from 3 to 14. Then, by 1881, the population had risen to 555, dropping to 419 by 1901.

In 1931 it was 404, rising to 892 in 1991 and to 903 in 2001.

Quarndon's overall population and housing figures have to be viewed alongside the boundary changes of 1974 and 1984 (see Chapter 7), but the mid-19th century population fluctuations would suggest (a) an over-dependence on agriculture and associated trades in Quarndon, and (b) the later "pull" of employment attractions in the developing industries in and around Derby.

Since the turn of the 20th century, however, the village has attracted a marked influx of professional and business residents (what the local historian, Roy Christian, called "prosperous fugitives from Derby"!) and with it a corresponding increase in pre- and post-World War 2 housing. Since 1901, this has increased from 95 houses to today's figure of 379.

Framework knitting

Photo: David Widdows

Former framework knitting shop behind *The Quandary*

The Editor is grateful to Rosemary Lucas and Linda Owen for the following research.

In 1841, there were 17 silk framework knitters in the village - 13 of them heads of households. A framework knitting shop - now converted into a private house - stands at the back of what is now *The Quandary*, 100 Church Road. (See also Chapter 16.)

Of the other 94 heads of households, 31 were agricultural labourers, 16 were of independent means, 11 were farmers, 8 were joiners and the other 28 were variously employed in trades or professional occupations.

According to the accompanying literature to the flat bed framework knitting machine on display at Belper North Mill:"Derbyshire specialised in silk stockings and much of the industry was home-based. Hosiers provided the silk and rented the frames to the framework knitters, or 'stockingers'."

As Rosemary Lucas points out: "The framework knitting industry provided silk stockings for men wearing knee-length breeches, but, as the century progressed, the fashion for breeches moved to full-length trousers and the stocking industry declined. By 1851, the number of framework knitters was down to 14; by 1881, only 2 were left (both being over 70) and, by 1891, the industry had completely disappeared."

Photo: M Pitt. Courtesy: Belper North Mill Trust

Flat bed framework knitting machine

The Hampshire family: their trades & employees

*The Execrs of the late
A W. Richardson Esqr.*

QUARNDON, near Derby, _____ 18 /1

Dr. TO CHARLES HAMPSHIRE,

JOINER, BUILDER, WHEELWRIGHT, PAINTER, PAPERHANGER, &c., &c.

Hampshire employees

As is explained in Chapter 9, the Hampshire family - apart from running *The Joiners' Arms* - conducted their business of builders, joiners, wheelwrights, painters and decorators, blacksmiths, etc, in the grounds of the *Joiners'*. Among those who served their apprenticeship with the Hampshires were Arthur Heathcote and Bert German.

THE FORGE, QUARNDON,

Nr. DERBY,........................ ....195....

M... ......

Dr. to ARTHUR HEATHCOTE

SHOEING & GENERAL SMITH

Monthly Accounts

Arthur Heathcote: Blacksmith

Photos: Derby Evening Telegraph

Arthur Heathcote: Postman

Arthur Heathcote was the village blacksmith, chimneysweep, handyman and postman. He lived at 101 Church Road and had served his apprenticeship with the Hampshire family in the grounds of *The Joiners' Arms*.

As his son, Arthur, recalled:

"My father, son of the village hedgecutter, was Quarndon's blacksmith for over 50 years. His work included 'hooping' (burning the steel rim onto a wheel) with Bert German, the wheelwright [see *below*]. A 'Jack-of-all-trades', he was a real handyman - on call for anyone - repairing farm implements, chimney-sweeping, haircutting, taking a horse to plough. He also became the village postman from 5 to 10.30 am, then worked on other jobs until 10 at night."

To which Ivan Cope added: "Arthur Heathcote was the possessor of an elaborate extended ladder (very heavy and controlled by ropes), used for damson-picking. This was a thriving local industry, damson-trees being a regular feature in cottage gardens. The dye would be sold to the mills at Matlock and Stevensons at Ambergate. The remaining fruit would be made into preserves."

James Richardson, who spent his childhood at *Quarndon Hill*, has lasting memories of Arthur Heathcote as both chimney sweep and blacksmith.

"When he came to sweep the sitting room chimney, he would arrive on his black bicycle with the brushes and rods tied to the cross bar. The big window would be opened and, with the help of Frank, the gardener, the carpet would be rolled up and carried out on to the lawn. Mr Heathcote would then get to work with his rods. Like all small children, I would go outside, jump with excitement when I saw the brush emerge from the chimney-pot and rush in to tell him. Then down came the rods. He was now black from head to foot and the room was thick with soot. It had to be cleaned and the carpet unrolled on the lawn. This was beaten and tea leaves were scattered on it. It was then brushed with a stiff yard-broom. (The tea leaves were supposed to attract the dirt and the stiff brushing would fetch the dust from the pile - as recommended in Mrs Beeton's *Book of Household Management*). The carpet would then be rolled up again and returned to the sitting room.

I used to walk to his forge, and, if you were good, he'd let you pump the bellows. I'd watch him hammering a piece of steel into a horseshoe. One day, I admired one he'd just made and, in trying to pick it up, burnt my fingers. All he said was: 'That'll teach you to meddle with things without asking!'"

John Doman, a wartime evacuee (see Chapter 29), recalls: "I spent many hours with old Mr Heathcote, the blacksmith, listening to his stories, and, to this day, I can still ring the hammer on the anvil as he taught me."

Bert German

Bert German

Bert German was the village wheelwright, joiner and coffin-maker, employed by the Hampshires over the Smithy in the grounds of *The Joiners' Arms* from 1911 to 1925.

On 7th December, 1959, he and his wife, both aged 92, celebrated their 75th Wedding Anniversary. On that occasion he said: "We can recall many ups and downs - in peace and war, scarcity and prosperity - but we are pleased to know that we have not been a burden to our children... We count our blessings in having all good children, and children's children, and children's children's children." He died in 1961, aged 96.

The Richardson Vault

Following the death, in 1871, of William Richardson (of the leather tanning company), a family vault - which still exists today - was built in the Old Churchyard.

The invoice from Charles Hampshire states that the work involved lining it with 2,700 bricks.

It took just over 20 working days to complete and cost £11 10s 11d.

Arthur Heathcote, "Senior, Senior"

Arthur Heathcote, "Snr, Snr"

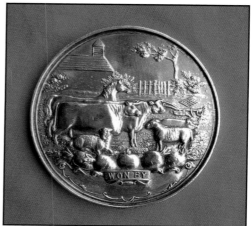

"King's Seedsmen" medal

Photos: Don Hall. Courtesy: Michael Heathcote

Arthur Heathcote (father of the aforementioned village blacksmith and postman) was Quarndon's champion hedgecutter. His (undated) medal was presented by the firm of Toogood & Sons, "The King's Seedsmen".

Bill Beeby: village coachman & coal merchant

LIVERY STABLES,
QUARNDON.
NR. DERBY, _May_ 1922

Miss Atkinson for Mrs Richardson

Dr. to W. T. BEEBY,
CAB PROPRIETOR.
COAL :: DEALER :: AND :: CARTER.

Bill Beeby

Bill Beeby worked from the Livery Stables (a former framework knitting shop) behind _The Quandary_ (see Chapter 16).

Referred to locally as "a colourful, good-natured character with a whistle and a ready smile", he would be up at 4am to fetch coal from Derby, after which he would drive his bus. When Kedleston School closed, he brought the eight children to Quarndon School in all weathers. According to Maurice Oakley: "Bill Beeby's Stage Coach conveying the schoolchildren from Kedleston to Quarndon and back was like a scene from a Western movie! He would also charge five shillings to take passengers in his bus from Derby to Dovedale & return."

Bill Beeby's daughter, Mary Jepson (who, incidentally, is said to have had a beautiful singing voice, and was a leading light in between-the-wars Church Hall productions) said of her father:

"Beeby's Ten Mile Drive" (through Kedleston Park)

"He owned two wagonettes, one Victoria, one brougham, one dog-cart and a smaller vehicle. The famous 'Beeby's Ten Mile Drive' was from the Tram Terminus on the Kedleston Road, Derby (near the present entrance to Derby University), up through Kedleston Park, by Park Nook and _The Black Cottage_ - where they'd stop for a cup of tea - then back home via Allestree Lane, where children would open the gates. My father drove a bus into Derby twice a week on market days. He also broke in horses."

Arthur Heathcote (Jnr) added:

"There was nothing 'BB' didn't know about a horse. He had a friend at *Park Nook Farm* and would often abandon roads and ride his horse over the fields and hedges to get there more quickly. He was also noted for his unmistakeable laugh - it could last for ten minutes! He'd once worked as an ostler at the *Royal Hotel*, Derby. One of the guests at the hotel was someone with the stage name "Little Titch", who was currently appearing at the Derby Hippodrome. From his window he could hear Bill laughing in the yard. So he challenged him: 'If you can stop my show with your laughing there'll be 50 bob for you.' (In those days that was a week's wages!) They sat him in the back row and he started to laugh. The more people looked round, the more he laughed! He was hauled out and paid the fifty bob - the only man who stopped a show for laughing!

On one occasion, he fell off a haystack. His family sent for the doctor, who arrived the following day. But BB had left at 4 that morning. On his way back, half way up the hill, the doctor met Bill returning with his coal from Derby. 'Don't bother coming to see me till I pass away,' said Bill. 'I'll send for ye when I need thee!'

Alas, he met his end falling off his horse on the Wirksworth Road. They think his horse must have turned right to go home via Cumberhills, while BB intended to carry straight on for a drink at *The White Hart*, Duffield. As a result, he was thrown, hit his head on the pavement and died in the Royal Infirmary on 30th March, 1922."

Apparently, his widow, Blanche, continued the carrier business until World War 2.

Quarndon bricks & brick-making

Photos: David Widdows

As the picture on the *left* illustrates, Quarndon bricks - some of them 400 years old - are characterised by being riddled with pebbles. The picture on the *right* is a detail of a wall in old farm buildings at 31 Church Road.

Apart from the existence of a field called Brick Kiln Close by Bunkers Hill, we know that a brickyard existed in a field called Stones Griff (No. 153 on *Field Map*, page 38) on a bend of The Common, opposite *Snowdrop Cottage*, 82 The Common.

Quarndon's Post Offices

The Editor is indebted to Harold S Wilson of Littleover and Frank Stone for the following information.

In 1846, the number of letters reaching Darley, Allestree and Quarndon amounted to 264 a week. So, on 23rd October that year, the Postmaster General announced that an official post was to be established from Derby. (Previously, the area had been served by an unofficial post operated by the Postmaster at Derby, with a charge for delivery.) This involved the employment of a messenger for 12 shillings a week and a receiver at Quarndon at £4 a year. In 1873, Quarndon's Post Office became a Sub Post Office under Derby and was able to issue and cash Money Orders.

In January, 1901, a day mail delivery service was established, with two deliveries on weekdays and one on Sundays. Before that, letters could be collected from the Post Office.

Until the mid-1960s there were no house numbers in Quarndon.

The original Post Office was at **Holly Bank**, Church Road (before the former garages were built).

Former garages, *Holly Bank*

Photo: David Widdows

The site today

Courtesy: Rod Jewell Collection

Church Road Post Office (No.115)

115 Church Road today

105 Church Road today

It is then said to have moved to what is now **No. 115 Church Road**; then to **No. 105**.

Later, it moved to what is now **Mulberry House** on The Common.

The Post Office on The Common

Mulberry House today

Finally, it moved to **Quarndon Stores**, (the former Wesleyan Chapel - see Chapter 15) on Church Road. The **Stores, Off Licence & Post Office** closed in 1997. It then became a private house.

Photo: Derby Evening Telegraph

Photo: Derby Trader

Photo: Don Hall

Former Stores, Off Licence & Post Office

Gordon & Eileen Warrington

The site today

Gordon & Eileen Warrington took over *Quarndon Stores* in 1984. Eileen says: "I persuaded Gordon into buying it. We learnt how to boil ham and it was a great success. Also Gordon used to get up at 4 or 5 in the morning and go down to the wholesale market to buy fresh vegetables. We wanted to go up-market and create a Fortnum & Masons on a smaller scale. So, for instance, we stocked Epicure food and Tiptree jams. As for any goods past their sell-by-date, that was a nightmare. We wouldn't sell them, but lived on out-of-date food - and were very healthy! However, we did notice a big drop in business when Sainsburys opened on Kingsway. Then, in 1991, when Gordon died suddenly, I put the *Stores* on the market. Our successors incorporated the Post Office when it closed on The Common, but the *Stores, Off Licence & Post Office* closed in 1997."

The Black Cottage

Photo: Don Hall

Woodlands Lane elevation

This was occupied by Tom Handley (see also Chapter 26), gardener to the Anns of *Quarndon House* on The Common. In a corrugated iron shed, painted red, Tom's wife and mother ran a teashop - also selling tobacco, parkin (moist, spicy ginger-cake, usually containing oatmeal) and sweets. They also replenished hikers' billycans.

According to Frank Stone: "For a penny you could buy ginger beer or five caramels."

Ivan Cope added: "The theory that a former Lord Scarsdale had the building painted black, so that his view of it from Kedleston merged in with the trees, is not true. (But he did insist that the roofs of the former police houses in Woodlands Lane be green!) The 4.5-inch walls of the *Black Cottage* were pitched to protect them from damp and rain."

Photo: Rosemary Lucas

***Black Cottage* garden (Former red shed on *left*)**

No. 101 Church Road

101 Church Road: before the rendering of the east wall

101 Church Road: after rendering

This was once a **Butcher's Shop**.

In the picture on the *left* (taken before the recent rendering of the street wall - see picture on *right*), the bow window is modern, but the darker areas of brickwork on the wall flush with the pavement show (from *left* to *right*) the positioning of the former shop window, the Royal Mail box and the front door.

Because the premises had no refrigerator or freezer, meat was sold at knocked-down prices on a Saturday night.

According to Maurice Oakley: "There's a story that Quarndon's butcher used to collect his meat with his pony and trap from Derby, but was repeatedly being robbed in the dark on the way home. One night he spotted the culprit in action and applied his cleaver. Result: the thief disappeared into the darkness minus two fingers!"

13. Village life

Cartoon illustrations by **PAMELA COPESTAKE**

Every old village has its anthology of anecdotes and accounts - some oral, some written, some amusing, some sad - concerning characters, customs, events and everyday life. The Editor is indebted to Frank Stone, Derek Wigley, Mary Jepson, Brenda Ray, Diane Law and the late Ellen Hampshire, Arthur Heathcote (Jnr), Marjorie Sulley, Ivan Cope and others for the following recollections.

(a) People & places

(i) The Walking Fowkes

'Nanny' Fowke

'Collier' Fowke

An entry in *The Derby Mercury* of 8th August, 1849, announces the death "at Derby, on the 19th *ultimo*, in her 103rd year, of Mrs Annie Fowke, of Quarndon, with all her faculties." According to Ellen Hampshire, in her *History of Quarndon*:

> "Until she attained the age of 98, 'Nanny' Fowke had been employed by Mr Samuel Evans, banker, of Derby, in his gardens at Allestree Hall. In January, 1837, when over 90, she walked from Quarndon to London to attend the trial of her son, who was charged with assault. The trial took place at the Old Bailey and old Nanny completed her journey in five days, arriving in time to speak a good word for her boy, who was acquitted. Happily, she was spared the ordeal of walking back, Mr Evans paying her stage-coach fare."

She goes on:

> "Another member of the Fowke family, who lived in Quarndon, was a collier who walked to and from the pit at Eastwood daily, thus doing over 20 miles a day. He had to be at work at 6 in the morning, and, during winter, it was dark when he came out of the pit, so that he only saw daylight on Saturday afternoons and Sundays!"

(ii) Tom Shotton

Tom Shotton

Brenda Ray

Vine Cottage

"Tom Shotton was the village tailor, who had also worked for the General Post Office.

He sported a walrus moustache and wore a morning suit and spats. He was the Overseer of the Poor for 25 years and served on the Parish Council from 1901 to 1931. He was also a local Church Warden, who, during an interregnum in 1921, conducted 56 services! He also wrote regular reports for the *Derbyshire Advertiser.*

As his great-granddaughter, Brenda Ray, writes, Tom lived at *Vine Cottage* when it was indeed one cottage - lower in height and thatched (see painting by C Douglas Neal, *above left*). But she adds that his home life was clouded by three mysterious disappearances:

"In 1882, Thomas Forskut Shotton married Sarah Elizabeth Whieldon. They had two daughters, the second of whom - Maude - was my grandmother. But, eight days after Maude was born, her mother abandoned the family, never to return. Her disappearance was a great scandal and source of shame to the family. Thomas brought up the two daughters - helped for a time by his youngest sister, Polly. (She later married a feckless charmer, who went off to Canada prospecting - squandering much of her money en route - and never returned!)

Thomas and Sarah Shotton's other daughter, Florence, married Reg Hood, a local coachman. They had three children: Edna, Tommy and Florence. But in 1913, shortly after the birth of Florence, Florence (senior) died. Two years later, double tragedy hit the family when Reg was killed in the Dardanelles and Tommy died, aged 3. So Edna and Florence came to live with their grandfather - the said Thomas Shotton. Thus the former single parent became a single grandparent! But he did employ a housekeeper. Then in 1917, Florence (4) disappeared - abducted, it was believed, by the housekeeper. Neither was seen again."

Outside *Vine Cottage*, circa 1900
Left to right: **Maude (holding Ben, the horse); Tom Shotton (sitting on the trap);**
(Probably) Tom Whieldon, Tom Shotton's father-in-law (facing camera); Polly, Tom's younger sister (in profile).

Tom Shotton's other entry in the history books prompted this headline in the *Derby Daily Telegraph* of 12th April, 1930: "Quarndon Councillors find themselves in Quandary!" It concerned an Annual Meeting of the Parish Council Electors on 3rd April, 1930 - the minutes of which, and of a subsequent meeting, read as follows:

"Mr Shotton said that members of the Council had not signed Declarations of Acceptance of Office forms and that all business transacted by the present Council was null and void...The Clerk promised to make enquiries as to the law on these matters."

At the next Parish Council Meeting, on 11th April, 1930:

"Mr Hanley asked: 'Was this Council legally elected?' Mr Beeson amended the question to: 'Are the proceedings of this Council valid?' The Chairman replied in the affirmative....Mr Coy then pointed out that, according to the Minute Book, 'Acceptance of Office' forms had been signed once only during the past 20 years, namely in 1922, which statement was disputed by Mr Shotton, who claimed that such forms were signed in 1925.

After a long discussion, the Chairman proposed that the forms be signed now. Mr Beeson seconded the resolution, and, all being in favour, the 'Declaration of Acceptance of Office as Parish Councillor' forms were duly signed and witnessed. Mr Coy then asked: 'Are we satisfied that we are legal members of this Parish Council and have been so for the past two years?' In answer to this, Mr Shotton proposed 'That, having signed Acceptance of Office forms, we are all members of this Council from tonight.' Mr Coy moved an Amendment 'That the proceedings of this Council are valid and have been so for the last two years', taking as his authority the Local Government Act of 1894, 1st Schedule, Part 2, Rule 12. Mr Wood seconded the Amendment, which was put to vote. Mr Hanley and Mr Beeson were in favour, Mr Shotton against. The Amendment was therefore resolved."

Facsimile of Parish Council Minute, 11.4.30

(iii) Louisa Taft: The 'Village Eye'

Courtesy: Darren Marks

South View (date unknown)

South View today

According to Ivan Cope: "**Miss Taft** (*left*), who lived at *South View*, 121 Church Road, was the 'Village Eye'. She sat, hour after hour, looking out through the lace curtains at every movement up and down the road."

He added: "121 used to be three cottages. In the middle one - now a kitchen - lived a mother, father and nine children!"

(iv) Arthur & Bertha Stone

Arthur & Bertha Stone

Arthur & Bertha Stone (Frank's parents) lived at *The Myrtles*, No. 99 Church Road. Their granddaughter, Diane Law, writes: "My mother told me that, originally, *The Myrtles* had gas lights downstairs and the family used candles when they went upstairs to bed. After they had electricity installed, Arthur would still use a candle to go to bed, followed by Bertha, who would switch the light on!

One day, a message was left at *The Myrtles* for Arthur to go and see Mr Marsh, two doors up the hill. He had gangrene in his big toe and the doctor had told him his leg would have to be amputated. He didn't fancy that so he asked Arthur to operate on the offending toe. Arthur had been in the Veterinary Corps in the First World War and had always kept a sharp, bone-handled folding-knife in his pocket for attending horses and mules. He gave Mr Marsh a few drinks to dull the pain then cut off his toe. The patient lived, but the horrified doctor warned that, had Mr Marsh died within 12 months of the 'operation', my grandfather would have been charged with manslaughter!"

(v) Arthur Heathcote, Jnr

Photo: Derby Evening Telegraph

Church Road in the snow. (Date unknown.)

One authentic picture of village life in the early 20th century came from the late **Arthur Heathcote**, son of Arthur Heathcote, the village blacksmith, chimney sweep, barber, hedge-cutter and postman (see Chapter 12): "In 1922, there were only four cars in the village (one of them a 1921 'Tin Lizzy'). That winter, there was a heavy fall of snow, which wasn't cleared for three or four days. So, in the evening - once we'd checked that all four cars were in - we used to toboggan from the top of The Common down to Quarndon Turn. We intended to carry on doing this as long as the snow lasted, and it's a wonder we didn't knock anyone down! But one night we ended up under a policeman's nose at Quarndon Turn. He advised us to use the fields - so after that we did, down the slope behind *Montpelier Farm*.

Looking back to my childhood, we enjoyed our spare time and made the best of country life - playing football and cricket in the fields. The farmers never minded, and, in any case, we used to help them out when need arose."

(vi) Mary Jepson

Haymaking in Quarndon. (Date unknown.)

Another recollection came from the late **Mary Jepson** (daughter of Bill Beeby - see Chapter 12): "We had three hayfields (Beeby's Fields) on The Common, opposite *Snowdrop Cottage*. Before my brothers left for school in the morning, they had to fetch the horses, then take them back at night. During hay-making I was allowed to have a ride home on the hay-cart. I thought that was lovely. Happy times, weren't they, when you were young!"

(vii) Bertie Banks

Brenda Ray writes: "**Bertie Banks** was Quarndon's mystery poet - none of whose poems, alas, has survived. He was a driver for the Trent Bus Company and was notorious for the fact that when he climbed into the driver's cabin, he always removed his shoes. This, he claimed, enabled him to have better control of the clutch, footbrake and accelerator! But perhaps his greatest claim to fame was that, during World War 1, he'd been Lawrence of Arabia's driver."

(viii) Woodlands Lane

In living memory, this was a gated - "limestone chatter" - bridle path. (At one point the painter of the street sign spelt it "bridal"!) One gate was by what is now the Water Tower and another was at the Car Park.

David Widdows (now of *The Laurels*, Church Road) writes: "In the 1930s I lived in the house opposite the Water Tower, then known as *Woodcote*. My sister and I often spent weekend afternoons opening the gate for passing motorists and would be thrown ha'pennies and pennies - which we could spend on sweets at *The Black Cottage*!" David also adds: "Beyond the Water Tower there were gravel-pits on either side of the road" [one of them used as the village refuse tip before Council collections] "hence some of the hills and dales in Allestree Park, which were used for slit trenches, rifle ranges and tank training during World War 2."

According to Frank Stone, the road was famous for its avenue of mature beech trees and achieved an outcry in the national press in 1941 when they were all felled to construct the wooden frames of Mosquito bombers. Frank also adds that turf from the farm where the Water Tower now stands was transferred to the pitch at the Baseball Ground - former home of Derby County Football Club.

(ix) Barn Close

This was originally a field of that name, where the (four-day) Whitsun Territorial Camp was held - Major Eardley Simpson of *The Grange* taking the salute on the Sunday morning.

(x) Cannon Hill

(Nos. 94, 95 & 112 on Field Map, page 38)

   At times of national emergency - such as the Spanish Armada, the Napoleonic threats and famine riots in the 19th century - it's said that a cannon was trundled out from *Kedleston Hall* to the top corner of Cannon Hill to guard the turnpikes from Shardlow to Brassington.

(xi) The "Royal" Scarsdale Lodge

According to Ellen Hampshire:

"In 1845, the late Mr Charles Hampshire, of *The Joiners' Arms*, started a club [long since disbanded] for the benefit of the working men in Quarndon. It was to be known as 'The Loyal Scarsdale Lodge of the Grand United Order of Odd Fellows'. The printer, however, made a mistake and, instead of the word 'Loyal' printed 'Royal', and so it remained 'The Royal Scarsdale Lodge'. It was always the custom to assemble on Whit Wednesday at *The Joiners' Arms*. After being attired in their regalia, they marched in procession, with two of their members carrying their beautiful banner and headed by the Quarndon Brass Band - in their blue uniforms with gold trimmings - to the Church, where a service was held. After the service, they marched all round the village and returned to *The Joiners' Arms*, where dinner was served."

(b) 20th & 21st century Organisations

(For up-to-date information on the following, you're invited to visit: **www.quarndon.parishcouncil.net**
Current information welcomed by e-mail on: **enquiries@quarndon.parishcouncil.net***)*

(i) St Paul's, Quarndon, Mothers' Union

Founded: February, 1932. First enrolling member: Mary Adams, wife of Canon Francis Adams, first Secretary of the Derby Diocese (see Chapter 19). The aims of the movement are: "To uphold Christ's teaching on the nature of marriage and promote its wider understanding; to encourage parents to bring up their children in the faith and life of the Church; to maintain a worldwide fellowship of Christians, united in prayer, worship and service; to promote conditions in society favourable to stable family life and the protection of children, and to help those whose family life has met with adversity."

The gold Branch Banner (*top left*), made by Brenda Marchbank, depicts the Virgin & Child. It was dedicated at the Duffield Deanery Service held in St Paul's Church, Quarndon, on 26th September, 1979. It hangs in a glass case in the St John's Chapel near the door of the Church. Pictured *top right* is the St Paul's MU display in the Quarndon Millennium Flower Festival held in Church in July, 2000. Sadly, due to decreasing numbers, the Branch was disbanded in December, 2007. 12 years before it had been instrumental in the foundation of the Edward Bear Club.

(ii) Edward Bear Club

Edward Bear Club's first meeting, 1995 (Kay Morison *far left*).

Founded: September, 1995, by the Rev'd John Morison, the then Vicar of Quarndon, and his wife, Kay. The Club is open to pre-school children and their parents, grandparents and carers. There is no charge.

Until the St Paul's, Quarndon, Mothers' Union disbanded in December, 2007, it enjoyed their full support and is still helped by former members. It meets in Church every Thursday in term time from 2.15 to 3.30pm. This is meant as a "good first experience of Church for the children, where they have free access to all parts of the building, except the Altar". A short Service is followed by playtime and refreshments and there is a small lending library on the front pew.

(iii) Facts Club

Founded: 2002 by Alistair & Sue Kennedy as a Friday After School Club. It then moved to the first and third Sunday mornings in term time at 10 o'clock in the Village Hall.

Its aims are to tell the Christian story in a way appropriate to each child's age and development; provide a safe, caring and friendly environment, where children can explore aspects of Christianity; plan activities whereby children can have fun and enjoy being together.

Highlights have included a holiday club - *The Potting Shed* - in 2003 and a *Talent Show* in March, 2008.

**Children's Banner
(front)**

**St Francis of Assisi
(back)**

(iv) SPY Club (St Paul's Youth Club)

Founded: January, 2006, by Helen Latham for 10- to 14-year-olds. It usually meets from 7 to 9 pm on the first Saturday of the month in the Village Hall. Activities include table tennis, Pool, playstation games, table football and a tuck shop. Highlights have included a Pizza & Movie Evening and a Great Egg Challenge Evening. During the session there's usually a discussion on a chosen topic. Funds have been raised for a Christian Aid community tap and there have been visits to Alton Towers and Megabowl.

(v) Quarndon Ladies' Guild

Founded: October, 1959, under the Chairmanship of Eileen (wife of the then Vicar, Canon Alan Andrews). Members take care of the Church altar linen; they also clean the brasses and deal with the previous week's altar flowers. The Chairman hosts two formal meetings a year and several informal meetings are held at members' homes. The Guild will celebrate its half century in October, 2009.

(vi) Allestree Churches Together

This exists to further ecumenical relations between the Anglican, Roman Catholic, Baptist and Methodist Churches and Woodlands Chapel in the Quarndon, Allestree and Darley Abbey area. It organises such events as *Lent Study Groups, Good Friday* and *Christmas Open Air Services* at Park Farm, an *Advent Quiet Evening* and various activities during the Week of Prayer for Christian Unity.

To support the work of the Church of North India, an Allestree partnership with the Social Services Institute in Nagpur was set up 25 years ago, but is now a separate organisation. Fund-raising lunches are organised during Saturdays in Lent - each one hosted by a different Church - and open evenings are held once or twice a year to inform people about the work going on in Nagpur and the problems there.

(vii) Quarndon Pre-School (Lower Village Hall)

Founded: About 40 years ago by Lindsay Slater of Barn Close, to provide care and education for children aged 2 to 5 years. The group began by opening two mornings a week, but now runs for five days, during school term time. 20 children attend between 9 am and 1 pm. In 2004 the group was awarded a *Pre-School Accreditation Quality Assessment*, and, the same year, received an *Aiming for Quality* certificate from Derbyshire County Council.

(viii) 1st Quarndon Brownies

Founded for girls aged 7 to 11 years. Three years ago it was re-started after a short break. It currently has 22 members and meets - in school term time - on Wednesdays, from 6 to 7.30 pm in the Village Hall.

(ix) Quarndon Ladies' Club

In the early 1970s, Canon Alan Andrews, the then Vicar, suggested to Gretchen Smith that the young women of Quarndon should form a social group. She and others set up "Quarndon Young Women's Club", with an age limit of 40, and at least 50 came to the first meeting. The Club supported Church fund-raising, local celebrations of the Queen's Silver Jubilee and the annual Garden Fête. It also organised footpath inspection walks as well as talks, demonstrations, quiz nights and barn dances. In time, the age limit was dropped and the name changed to "Quarndon Ladies' Club". It still arranges talks and, in addition, organises visits to gardens, restaurants and the theatre. It meets at 8.00 pm in the Village Hall on the first Monday of the month.

(x) *Quarndon Events*

Founded: 2002 by Tony Glover and others as *Q'Spire* to raise funds for the repair of the Church spire and, subsequently, for the extension and refurbishment of the Village Hall. For this it raised a total of £93,300. It later changed its name to *Team Events, Quarndon (TeQ)* and is now simply called *Quarndon Events*. Its aims are to promote social activity in the village and thereby raise funds for village amenities.

(xi) Quarndon Neighbourhood Watch

Founded: Late 1990s by Derek Kenworthy. Its purpose is to assist the village community by working with Derbyshire Police and the Neighbourhood Watch Liaison Committee to reduce crime. Initially it was organised by a 'telephone tree' system, but now e-mails are used as the main medium of communication.

(xii) Quarndon Conservative Coffee Club

Founded: 1980 by local residents to give support - by fund-raising where needed - to the Conservative Association. (The local MP at the time of publication is the Rt Hon. Patrick McLoughlin.) Members meet on the third Thursday morning of most months at a member's home.

(xiii) Quarndon Women's Institute

Photo: Ann Ousley

Quarndon Women's Institute's 87th Birthday Lunch, 19th March, 2008

Founded: 26th January, 1921, at a meeting in the (then) "Parish" Hall, when 35 members of the audience became members. The following month membership rose to 65. Today the figure is 20. Since that time meetings have taken place in various halls, including the - now demolished - "Tabernacle" (among the former workshops in the grounds of *The Joiners' Arms*), the Wesleyan Chapel, *The Quandary*, the Quarn Drive Free Church Schoolroom and, currently, in the Village Hall, where they began.

Among its members over the years have been a County Chairman, a County Vice-Chairman and a County Treasurer. It celebrated its 80th Birthday in 2001. Their Millennium Collage Wall Chart of Village Activities hangs in the Village Hall (see Chapter 32). The framed picture of the Chalybeate Spring, which hangs over the mantelpiece in the Hall, was presented by Quarndon WI.

(xiv) Quarndon Men's Luncheon Club

Founded: 22nd January, 1998, by David Widdows and John Banham "to promote good chat, good ale and good food for men living in Quarndon".

It meets at the *Joiners' Arms* at 12 for 12.30 on the last Thursday of every month, except in December.

(xv) Quarndon Autumn Leaves Club

25th Anniversary, 1990, in the Village Hall

Founded (it's believed) in 1965, its objects are: "To provide a meeting place and recreational facilities and pursue any objects which now are, or hereafter may be deemed by law to be, charitable for the benefit of the elderly people who live in Quarndon."

Among those who were instrumental in forming the Club was the late Canon Alan Andrews, Vicar of Quarndon, 1958-1979. Another was the late Gina Richardson, of *Quarndon Hall,* who - until cheap package tours became popular - organised well-supported holidays by the sea. She also hosted the annual strawberry tea and led the Club for many years.

Sylvia Widdows, who ran the Club from 1983 to 2008, writes: "A traditional Christmas Lunch continues to this day and several parties are held during the year. Meetings are held twice a month in the Village Hall and there is often a speaker. Twice a year a coach trip is organised to a place of interest, including lunch or tea. Membership has declined over the years, but the Club survives with a nucleus of loyal members and a band of willing helpers."

(xvi) Lesley's Wednesday Workout

Founded: 1988 by Lesley Kirkland. Its aims are to improve fitness levels and have fun at the same time. It meets at 9.15am every Wednesday in term time in the Village Hall.

Top: Old Croft House as a School   Bottom: Old Croft House today

14. Quarndon's schools

*(The Editor wishes to thank **BRIAN WINDSCHEFFEL** - former Head Teacher, the Curzon Church of England, Voluntary Aided, Primary School - for the loan of Head Teachers' Logs, School Managers' Minutes and school photographs.)*

OVER nearly 300 years, schooling in Quarndon has taken place in a variety of premises. The first school was established following the death of Sir John Curzon of Kedleston, 3rd Baronet, in 1727. In his Will, dated 10th May, 1725, he left "£20 per annum for the education of twenty poor children of Kedleston, Quarndon, Weston Underwood and Ravensdale Park". The Headmaster, who was to be in Holy Orders, would receive £16 per annum, plus £4 to buy books, paper, pens and ink for the children. He was required to instruct them in reading, writing and accounts. He would also receive £10 per annum to read prayers and preach in Quarndon Chapel. Later it was stated that the Master "take at least twenty poor children who are appointed by Lord Scarsdale from Quarndon, Kedleston and the Parish of Mugginton and instruct them in reading, writing and accounts without any charge; he may also take boarders and other children who pay for their education".

Courtesy: The Curzon (C of E) Primary School

School photograph (1922) during the headship of Robert Rylatt (*top left*)

The School building - now *Old Croft House*, 23 Church Road (see *opposite*) - was described as consisting of "a good dwelling, house and garden, with a small croft and playground, in all rather more than an acre". This was later extended to accommodate 30 fee-paying boarders.

Later still, it became a boys' boarding school "Entrance: One Guinea[£1.1s]; Board & Commercial Education: 21 Guineas per Annum; Instructions in the Greek, Latin or French Languages: One Guinea per Quarter; Dancing & Drawing, by approved Masters, on the usual Terms; Washing & Mending: Two Guineas per annum." Finally, it became a girls' finishing school, which closed in 1889.

Meanwhile, in 1859, the **Rev'd Alfred, 4th Baron Scarsdale** (*right*), established a charity for "regulating and directing the administration of a School" to be built next to land now occupied by St Paul's Church.

Records show that on 13th November, 1861, the sum of £300 was received from Lord Scarsdale "in account of building the new school".

Scarsdale Collection, Kedleston Hall, The National Trust

4th Baron Scarsdale

Courtesy: Curzon Papers, Kedleston Hall

The architect's original concept of the 1861 School

The actual (1861) School building. Demolished in 1967 - except for the *School* (Headmaster's) *House* (right). Note the Girls' Gable Entrance (*far left*) and the Boys' Gable Entrance (*right*).

Left: The present School, which replaced the old building. *Right: The School House -* now a tenanted property on the Kedleston Estate. (Note the gable imprint left from the former Boys' Entrance on the wall.) *Centre:* the 1861 Scarsdale crest over the *School House* door.

Headmasters' Logs for the school present a reflection of the seasonal rhythms and demands of rural life. In the latter part of the 19th century children were kept away because of "stone-picking for farmers", "to go begging", "assisting their parents preparing for Whitsuntide", "hay-harvesting", "gathering herbs", "fruit-picking" and "because of a large sale at a gentleman's house".

In the early years of the Victorian school the Vicar is repeatedly recorded as helping parents who fell into arrears with their fees - in 1881 these being 2d per week, or 3d for a higher grade. There are also allegations of harsh discipline at the school. In the Spring of 1885, it was alleged: "Miss Ashton beat William on the knuckles until they bled - also on the head because he cannot do his sums", and: "Thomas was beaten till he was black and blue from the elbow to the wrist".

Robert Rylatt

Robert Rylatt was the headmaster from 1890 to 1924. He often received serious complaints from irate parents. One father is recorded as accusing him of pocketing his son's fee (although this was never taken seriously by the authorities). There are references to boys being "spoken to on the duty of showing kindness and respect to girls everywhere" and of "severe punishment" being administered to a boy for "immoral talk to a girl", plus a recommendation that "he be dismissed should it ever occur again".

Disease was often a major cause of low attendance. Scarlet fever closed the school for the last eight weeks of 1895; measles closed it for seven weeks in 1905 and the entry for 22nd October, 1915, reads like a visitation of doom: "Scarlet Fever is in this Village. Doris Bull, an Infant of this School, died of it on Monday last. Agnes Williams has since been taken to the Fever Hospital suffering from it. I have this afternoon sent home Mavis Burton who was poorly and I should not be surprised if she also has contracted it."

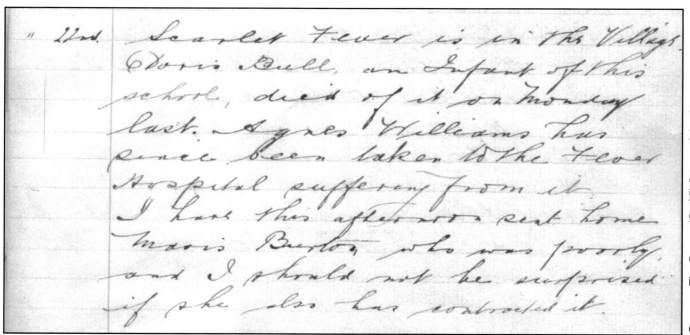

Courtesy: The Curzon (C of E) Primary School

Log facsimile

Half a century later, because of an influenza outbreak in January, 1966, only 12 out of 42 children attended school.

Severe weather - for example, "heavy snow", "downfalls of rain" and "37 degrees of frost" - caused heavy absenteeism. On 18th January, 1912, the Log states: "29 out of 72 children attended school today on account of the snow storm and depth of snow".

National issues and festivities also feature in the Logs. 1st January, 1894: "A new Act comes into force today which states that no child can be legally employed - either as half or whole timer - unless such a child is 11 years of age." Medals were issued to commemorate Queen Victoria's Golden Jubilee in 1887 and, ten years later, a week's holiday was granted for her Diamond Jubilee. There were also special holidays of varying lengths to celebrate the wedding of the Duke of York (the future King George V), the Relief of Mafeking, "the return of the Derby Volunteers from the Transvaal War", the termination of the 1914-18 War, the signing of the Treaty of Versailles, coronations, royal visits and jubilees, and "so that the children may see Barnum & Bailey's Great Street Procession in Derby".

For years the Hon. Mrs Harriet Jervis of *Quarndon Hall* gave the children "an annual treat at her house" and, in 1902, Captain Alfred Jacobson is recorded as having "invited the children to his residence [*Quarndon Hill*] on Christmas Eve to see a Cinematograph entertainment and to have tea".

In later years Lord Scarsdale gave £5 from the Foundation Manager's Fund towards a children's treat at Dale Abbey (1923); £2 for an outing to Belle Vue (1947) and 2 guineas for a trip to Skegness (1948).

In 1909 the seven children attending Kedleston School were transferred to Quarndon School. Electric light was fitted in 1912. A school inspection carried out on 18th December, 1914, found that arithmetic was "unsatisfactory in Standards II & III", spelling was "weak in the senior class", but written English was "making good progress". That same year the "closets" had been "converted into a water carriage system" and the Log for 22nd May, 1916, states: "The Daylight Saving Measures came into force yesterday and the clocks were advanced one hour."

From Day One the Logs record the regular visits made to the School by its founder, the 4th Baron Scarsdale (see page 96) - the last being three months before his death. The entry for 2nd December, 1915, reads: "Lord Scarsdale called this afternoon, but was unable to leave his carriage." Then, on 23rd March, 1916: "Lord Scarsdale, the Chairman of the School Managers and Trustee of this School, died 2.30 pm today."

In 1917 Robert Rylatt suffered "a complete breakdown in health" and was ordered three months' extra holiday by his doctor. In 1919 a schools inspector recommended that "arithmetic throughout the senior department of the school should receive special attention; its practice should be less formal in character and should be more closely connected with the problems of everyday life".

But, in 1922, the school managers applied to the County Council Education Committee for an increase in the Headmaster's salary "in consequence of the satisfactory nature of the last HM Inspector's Report and the general tone, order and discipline of the School".

However, correspondence shows that, after his retirement, Rylatt was reluctant to leave the *School House*. In a letter to the Vicar, dated 31st December, 1924, the agent for the Kedleston Estate wrote: "He has had years to get a house, and I should certainly myself use all powers to get him out!"

Photo: Derby Evening Telegraph

George Beeson (*left*) 2nd Viscount Scarsdale (*centre*) & the Rev'd Emmerson Richardson at a Prize-giving

Rylatt's successor, **George Beeson**, was headmaster from 1924-1949 (pictured on *left*). He has long been remembered with affection by former pupils.

One of them, the late Fred Kelsey, wrote: "Mr Beeson was a good teacher, but he suffered from the effects of being gassed in the War and sometimes his temper got the better of him. It was then woe betide any offender! But he was a man who could teach anything from music to gardening."

Frank Stone points out: "As evidence of George Beeson's ability as a teacher, during the period 1931 to 1936, eight pupils were successful in passing the grammar school examination to Derby or Belper Schools."

Maurice Oakley, formerly of *Burley Grange*, writes: "G H Beeson ('GHB') was a great headmaster, teacher and friend. He played football and cricket with the boys on Wednesday afternoons, taught every subject and only used the cane when necessary. Most of the kids thought the world of him! He had a greyhound that was said to be the pup of a former Waterloo (hare-coursing) Cup winner. He also drove a Morris Cowley with a 'dickie-seat' in the back."

Another ex-pupil tells of a group of class-mates who "lifted the Rev'd Emmerson Richardson's Austin 7 to 'relocate' it behind the Church Hall - for which they received the infamous cane".

Maurice Oakley continues: "When his wife died, Mr Beeson moved to South Devon. Years later, when I was down in that part of the world on holiday, I decided to look him up. I found the house, but there was no reply at the door. So I looked through the window and recognised a picture on the wall that used to hang in his lounge at the *School House* in Quarndon. I enquired in the village and they said: 'Sorry, we buried Mr Beeson last week.'"

According to Frank Stone:

"The old School had an open fire for the Infants and a form of central heating for the Juniors. There was a sliding partition between the two classes. The windows were six feet above the ground, so our attention was not diverted. There were segregated playgrounds and outside toilets."

Photo: *Derby Evening Telegraph*

Old School Infants' Classroom

The late Fred Kelsey wrote:

"Miss Ashton" [see page 98] "was a dear old lady. She was very strict and stern, but thought the world of us children. In the infants' room there was a big fireplace in which a huge fire would be burning. If we got to school wet because of the rain she would take off our wet clothes to dry by the fire. But if she caught you misbehaving she would put you across her knee and slap your behind with a ruler!"

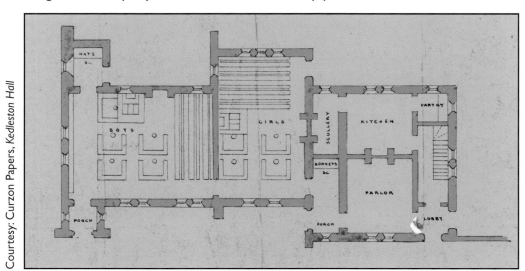

Courtesy: *Curzon Papers, Kedleston Hall*

Old School plan

The old School had two segregated classrooms: the room on the *left* (Boys) measuring 39 ft x 29 ft (11.9m x 8.8m) and the one in the *centre* (Girls), 39 ft x 23ft (11.9m x 7m).

Old School playground

Photo: Derby Evening Telegraph

In the *left* picture, Janice Kiernan (then an infants' teacher, standing in the far doorway), points out that the little boy looking (longingly?) over the wall from the *School House* garden is Mark Wibberley, the Headmaster's son - at 4 too young to attend school.

In 1967 the building - except the *School House* - was demolished. It was replaced by a new school, with teaching spaces arranged around a central activity area.

It opened on 4th September that year, and our picture, *left*, shows the children about to leave the old premises, taking with them the school bell.

Standing in the front row, *3rd* from *left*, is 5-year-old Heather Smith (now Whitworth), who recalls: "I remember the large main room in the old School, where it was either absolutely freezing or fuggy and hot. I used to cross my legs for as long as possible because the outside loos were so cold they

The move

Photo: Derby Evening Telegraph

sometimes froze up completely during the winter! As for the difference between the two buildings, there was the most amazing feeling of light and space in the new School. We had separate areas for each activity and much more room inside for displays, putting on performances, etc, and outside, where we could play and run around. I can remember PE and being fascinated by the sight and sound of the headmaster, Mr Wibberley, skipping - with the change in his trouser pockets rattling up and down!

Photo: *Derby Evening Telegraph*

Lunch in the new School Hall

School lunches also play a significant part in my early recollections - they were delicious!"

The new School was built to what was known as a "method-construction" design - the first of its kind in the Midlands. According to *The Architect & Building News* (13.12.67), the main aim of Method Building was "to provide a wider choice of structural solutions to satisfy local authority requirements and conditions, whilst at the same time enjoying the benefits of standardisation and factory-produced components". It also gave the architect "greater design freedom and a larger choice of materials in which to build. The school therefore has load-bearing brick walls, with modular facing bricks externally and fair-faced sand-lime bricks internally. Brick was chosen because it is a traditional material in the village." The total cost (including site-clearing) was £23,552.

Photo: *Derby Evening Telegraph*

The new School & outdoor play area

Anne Devenport - who introduced textile work skills to the school curriculum and was Deputy Head to Mr Wibberley and his two successors, as well as Acting Head, 1981-2, adds: "Reg Wibberley realised the unpleasant state of the outside toilets and asked initially for them only to be replaced.

The project then snowballed and ended up with the successful (albeit leaky-roofed!) building of the new school."

103

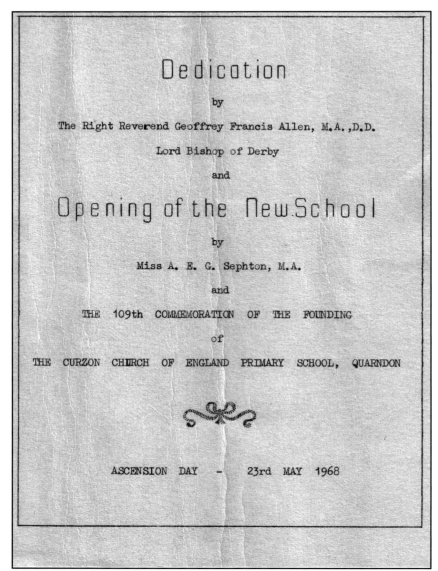

Dedication

by

The Right Reverend Geoffrey Francis Allen, M.A.,D.D.

Lord Bishop of Derby

and

Opening of the New School

by

Miss A. E. G. Sephton, M.A.

and

THE 109th COMMEMORATION OF THE FOUNDING

of

THE CURZON CHURCH OF ENGLAND PRIMARY SCHOOL, QUARNDON

ASCENSION DAY — 23rd MAY 1968

On Ascension Day (23rd May), 1968, the new "Voluntary Aided" School was dedicated by the then Bishop of Derby, the Rt Rev'd Geoffrey Allen, and officially opened by Amy Sephton, Principal of the then Bishop Lonsdale Training College (now Derby University). A Parent-Teacher Association was set up in 1977.

"Voluntary Aided" schools are managed locally and funded by the local education authority - in this case by Derbyshire County Council - with the majority of the Governors being nominated by the Parochial Church Council and appointed by the Diocesan Board of Education.

The aim is "to place the teaching of Jesus - 'to love God and your neighbour as yourself' - at the heart of children's values, work and relationships", with the Derby Diocese providing curriculum guidance and specialist advice. (In February, 1953, a strongly-worded note from the Diocesan Education Office stated that "the sands of time are running out with regard to the future status of Quarndon Parochial School". It warned that if application for 'Voluntary Aided' status were not made by April, it would automatically become a "Controlled" school, with the management in the hands of the County Council.)

Reg Wibberley

Reg Wibberley was Head Teacher from 1964-81. In 1967 he presided over the transition from the old school to the new one. When he retired, Canon Alan Andrews, who had been Chairman of the School Managers until 1979, wrote of him: "He realised at an early date that, apart from the poor conditions offered by the old building, the child population was increasing and the old school would be too small. Unless action had been taken at that time, it is probable that eventually the old school would have been closed and there would have ceased to be a Church School in Quarndon." In 1987 Reg Wibberley and Arthur Milroy (Chairman of the School Managers, 1979-1985) died within a few days of each other. Their funerals were on the same day.

Photo: *Derby Evening Telegraph*

Reg Wibberley's Retirement Party

Front row, far left: (Mrs) **Anne Devenport** (Deputy Head). To her *left*: (Mrs) **Kate Leather** (Textiles Adviser, Derbyshire County Council). *Centre* (holding gifts): **Reg Wibberley**. To his *right*: **Dennis Whittaker** (Area Education Officer, Amber Valley & Erewash). To Reg Wibberley's *left*: (Mrs) **Tassy Lichtarovizc** (Secretary, Parent Teacher Association); (Mrs) **Margery Sulley** (School Manager)*; (Mrs) **Ida Sherwin** (Cook); **Arthur Sulley** (School Manager)**; the **Rev'd Arthur Milroy** (Vicar of St Paul's, Quarndon, & Chairman of the Managers) and his wife **Ethel**.

Paul Clayton

Brian Windscheffel

During the headship of **Paul Clayton** (1982-89) the Annual School Foundation Commemoration Service was changed to a more modern one in which the pupils took a leading role. An Annual Christmas Concert at *Kedleston Hall* was also introduced.

A small extension, built on the back of the building, provided some extra teaching space and room for the School's first computers.

During the headship of **Brian Windscheffel** (1989-2006), the Curzon School - along with others - was given the responsibility of managing its own budget, and in 1994, the governors, with the support of parents, successfully applied for Grant Maintained status. This lasted until the return of a Labour Government in 1997.

Also that year the number of pupils passed the 100 mark. In 1998 a new classroom for the youngest children was built - coinciding with the introduction of nursery education.

*In 1982 Margery Sulley, a local JP and Chairman of Quarndon Parish Council from 1963 to 1966, co-wrote with Reg Wibberley: *Historical Vignettes of Quarndon*. **Arthur Sulley was MD of the Derby uniform manufacturers, James Smith. In 1974 he co-wrote (with H Hall): *Quarndon Parish Church & the Curzon Church of England School*. In 1928 & 1929 he'd coxed the Cambridge boat to victory against Oxford, and in 1928 was a member of the British rowing team which won the Silver Medal at the Amsterdam Olympic Games.

On the introduction of the National Curriculum (during Paul Clayton's headship), Brian Windscheffel said: "Accountability became the by-word and assessment was as much about gauging the performance of teachers as that of the pupils. Targets and league tables illustrated the climate in education around the turn of the Century."

In the year 2000 the School received an *Achievement Award* for its performance in national tests. The following year it achieved *Beacon School* status under which it acted as "a source of good practice and expertise for other schools". At the time of publication, the School has a teaching staff of 6.5 (including the head teacher) and 125 children on roll. It has five classrooms, including a 'temporary' one (though the intention is for it to become permanent). This was erected in the playground in 2004 to provide better learning conditions for 9-11 year-olds.

Geraldine Lowden

The current Head Teacher is **Geraldine Lowden**, who writes:

"With the introduction of the National Curriculum and the Qualifications & Curriculum Authority in 1988, teaching became rigidly prescribed. That's now changing, I'm glad to say! We've introduced cross-curricular work through themes - eg, studying World War 2 not just from history books, but through letters from servicemen and women. Staff and students find this method stimulating and interesting. There's also been an increase in after-school clubs, eg, country dancing, netball, art, computers and recorder-playing.

Another development has been a change in the dynamic of the teaching staff, bringing in two younger teachers in the first three years of their careers to complement the more experienced ones. The staff and parents have a good working relationship and have developed a superb outdoor area for children of all ages.

As for the challenges that lie ahead, by 2010 we must have established four hours a week of quality time PE for all ages (in the fight against obesity) as well as "wrap around" care for pupils from 8.00 am to 6.00 pm. Also, to help children reach their full potential, we should, as best we can, anticipate the changes they will experience. It's been said, for instance, that many of the jobs that will be available when our pupils leave school don't even exist at the moment! Added to which, the average child can expect to experience seven to nine career changes before he or she retires! We need to prepare our children to face this future as caring, responsible individuals."

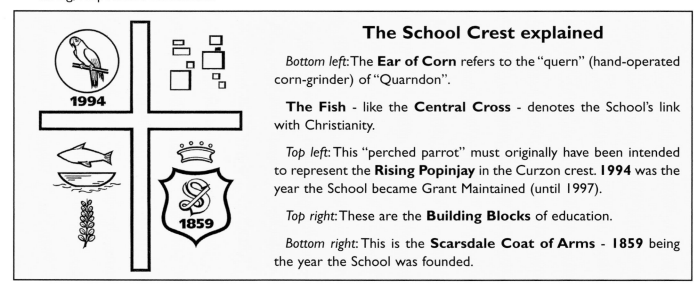

The School Crest explained

Bottom left: The **Ear of Corn** refers to the "quern" (hand-operated corn-grinder) of "Quarndon".

The Fish - like the **Central Cross** - denotes the School's link with Christianity.

Top left: This "perched parrot" must originally have been intended to represent the **Rising Popinjay** in the Curzon crest. **1994** was the year the School became Grant Maintained (until 1997).

Top right: These are the **Building Blocks** of education.

Bottom right: This is the **Scarsdale Coat of Arms** - **1859** being the year the School was founded.

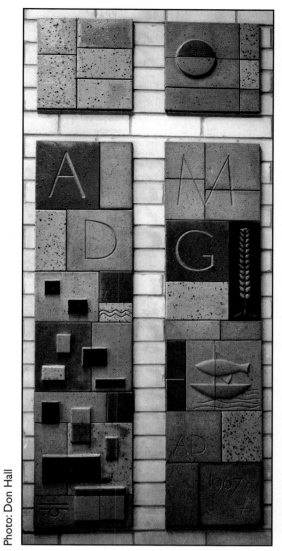

Photo: Don Hall

The Ronald Pope Sculpture
- in the School Hall, repeating many of
the emblems in the School Crest.

Well Dressing: "Jesus walks on the water"
- produced by pupils as part of Quarndon's Millennium Celebrations,
2000.

Head Teachers

William Thorpe	1824-1859	G H Beeson	1924-1949
Lawrence Thompson	1860-1862	Mrs H Rushton	1949-1963
Grace Chadwick	1864-1865	R A Wibberley	1964-1981
Miss Stanhope	1865-1876	P Clayton	1982-1989
Mr Young	1877-1890	B Windscheffel	1989-2006
R Rylatt	1890-1924	Mrs G Lowden	2007-

Photo: Derek Wigley

Two photographs of *Battelles Lane Barn.* (**Now demolished.**)

15. Methodists in Quarndon

By DON HALL

JOHN WESLEY, an Anglican priest whose life spanned much of the 18th century, was one of a group of Oxford students who formed a society referred to as "The Holy Club", or "Methodists" - so-called because of their methodical and austere way of life. From 1739 he travelled the country visiting poor neighbourhoods, where those who attended his meetings were mainly industrial or agricultural labourers.

As an evangelist Wesley persuaded people to work hard and save for the future; he had a lot to say about personal morality and he encouraged people to attend the local Anglican churches.

Methodists only separated formally from the Established Church after Wesley's death in 1791 - and against his wishes!

In Quarndon, from 1808 to 1866, the upper room of a farm building in Battelles Lane (now the bridleway from *Vine Cottage* on Church Road to *The Kedleston Hotel*) was used as a Meeting Room by Wesleyan Methodists ("to uphold Methodism in its original form - based on John Wesley's emphasis on 'a life of faith, self discipline and perfect love'").

The building - shown *opposite* in two stages of deterioration - has since been demolished.

In 1851 Joseph Allcock, a 32-year-old smallholder and joiner, moved to Quarndon with his wife, Mary, a laundress, and farmed two acres. They lived in a cottage on the site of the present Village Hall. Here Allcock and visiting preachers held meetings - first in one room, then in two adjacent rooms, with a specially-built rostrum between them. When this arrangement proved too small he built a chapel over the cowshed behind his house.

© National Portrait Gallery, London

John Wesley, by Nathaniel Hone.
(Oil on canvas, c 1766)

Joseph Allcock's house (with white window) is on the *right*. The Village Hall now occupies the site.

Photo: David Widdows

Plaque on Chapel portico

In time this, too, proved inadequate and, in 1859, at a cost of £300, a new, purpose-built Chapel, with School Room behind, was opened at what is now 116 Church Road. This was part of an ambitious and expensive nationwide programme of church and school building by the Wesleyan Methodists, resulting in an increase in membership from over 76,000 in 1791 to 285,000 in the late 1840s. The portico of the former Chapel still bears the inscription: "WESLEYAN CHAPEL 1859" (see *above*).

In the year it was opened services were held at 6.30 pm on Sundays, with, once a month, a further service being held on a Thursday evening. (Ivan Cope remembered the Minister at Quarndon's Chapel as "a big man, about six-foot-two and weighing 18 stone, who used to preach Hell-fire and damnation!")

Courtesy: Rod Jewell Collection

Wesleyan Chapel (*centre right* with portico), pre-1913.

Courtesy: Rod Jewell Collection

Wesleyan Chapel post-1913.
(The Institute - later Parish Hall, later Church Hall, now Village Hall - is in background.)

The Chapel was one of a "circuit" of 25 Wesleyan chapels - led from King Street Chapel (now demolished), which stood at the top of Chapel Street in Derby. There, children from Quarndon's Chapel were baptised and their names are to be found in the Baptismal Register (now at the Derbyshire Record Office, Matlock).

Joseph Allcock had been a typical reforming Methodist of his day, who prospered as a result of "thrift and clean living". *The Derby Electoral Register* lists him as a "£12 Occupier" (a householder who paid at least £12 in annual rent), who voted for the Liberal candidate in 1869. The 1881 Census lists his 18-year-old daughter, Elizabeth, as a pupil teacher. Nonconformists valued education as a means to a better life.

In 1884 Edward Kidger, a farmer, organised chapel meetings at 9.30 am on Sundays. He and his wife, Mary, lived with their eight children at *Bath Farm*, leasing 248 acres off the Kedleston Estate and employing five labourers. The family also had a governess and domestics. Chapel membership had now become respectable! At that time, nationally, nonconformists were more numerous than Anglicans and accounted for a third of worshippers.

At the turn of the 19th/20th century Wesleyan Methodists were each invited to donate one guinea to the Wesleyan Methodist Twentieth Century Fund to mark the centenary of John Wesley's death. Three local Chapel members, Eliza Bell, Miss M Ward (the Quarndon Postmistress) and Abraham Fowke (a 41-year-old joiner) are listed on the *Historic Roll* - a 50-volume, leather-bound record - as having contributed. The Fund raised £1,075,727 nationwide - £250,000 being allocated to erect the Central Methodist Hall, Westminster, which opened in 1912 as a world centre for Methodism.

(In 1946 it was the venue for the Inaugural Meeting of the General Assembly of the United Nations.)

For many years Quarndon's Chapel was the venue for *Mr Buxton's Library* - a collection of nearly 900 ("mainly classical") books.

In 1932 the Wesleyan Methodists amalgamated with two other Methodist factions - the Primitive and United Methodists - to form the Methodist Church of today. This meant that many chapel premises became redundant. Reductions in Methodist membership are also recorded - in 1933 there were only six adult members in Quarndon, sharing a full-time Minister with Ashbourne Road (Derby), Breadsall and Morley Moor Chapels.

During World War 2, because of difficulties in blacking out Quarndon's Chapel, services were held in a wooden hut in Quarn Drive, the Women's Institute using the Chapel for its afternoon meetings. (See Chapter 26: *Quarndon in Wartime - 1: The Home Front & "foreign field".*)

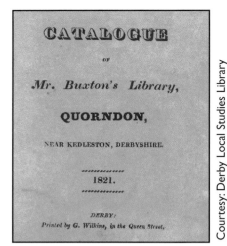

Courtesy: Derby Local Studies Library

Library catalogue: front cover

After the War, services resumed, but membership dwindled further and an increase in car ownership meant that people travelled to chapels with thriving congregations in more densely populated areas.

In 1958 Quarndon's Chapel was closed and sold for conversion to *The Quarndon Stores*. Later it became a private house.

In 2003 Methodist and Anglican Christians signed a "Covenant towards unity of thought and belief". John Wesley had been a very reluctant protester, a loyal conservative High Churchman and no natural rebel. Almost 150 years after Methodism began in Quarndon, separation of Anglican and Methodist has turned full circle with conversation towards unity.

Photo: *Derby Evening Telegraph*

Chapel building as *Quarndon Stores*

Photo: Don Hall

Chapel building today - as a private house

16. *The Quandary* (100 Church Road)

By *JONATHAN POWERS*

(The present owner-occupier)

The *Quandary*: before restoration & extension

The *Quandary*: today

THE name "Quandary" is presumably a play on the word "Quarndon", but the origins of this strange assortment of buildings - with its ten chimneys, nine different levels, three main staircases, 90-foot walk from front to back and bottle-shaped well - also pose a quandary for the historian! It certainly belies its appearance as a small cottage opening on to a village street.

Above: Former Coach House.
Below: **Converted to a private house.**

Photo: David Widdows

When the property came up for sale in 1992 the surveyor warned my bank that the building had "reached the end of its useful life and should be demolished"! (But then what are challenges for?) A later surveyor labelled it a "Tardis".

In the first quarter of the 19th century, a terrace of three, "one-up, one-down" cottages was constructed at right-angles to the road, together with a shared wash-house, earth closet and well. They swallowed an even older single-storey hovel.

A long building (*left*), at right angles to this terrace and parallel to the road, was built at the same time to accommodate a knitting-frame workshop. (See Chapter 12) This later became a coach-house (the name it bears today as a separate private house - see also *left*), first for the parish clerk and sexton, John Thomas Lowe, "hirer of cabs, hansoms, wagonettes and carriages", then for Bill Beeby, "cab proprietor, coal merchant and general carter", who lived in the main house. (Again, see Chapter 12.)

Remains of lintel sign

Half-sash window

During the reign of William IV (1830-37) *The King's Head* public house was built across the front of the properties. To accommodate this the cottage nearest the road was demolished and the materials re-used. (It is entertaining to note that the room which incorporates the remnants and footings of the vanished cottage is reputed by a number of villagers to be haunted by a ghost associated with the smell of lavender.)

Outside the inn sign is now lost, but a vestige of its licensing notice (see *above*) - which once read: "Licensed Refreshments. House-keeper and Bottler of BRITISH & FOREIGN WINES" - can be discerned on the lintel above the doorway,

According to Ellen Hampshire *The King's Head* was used as the Lodge House of the Quarndon Druids. But, at some time in the 1870s, the public house ceased to trade as such. The freehold was obtained by the Kedleston Estate and the rent was paid twice yearly. The original owner, Thomas Neal, sold the freehold to the Kedleston Estate in 1867 for £400.

The King's Head brewed beer on stone thrawls in the brick, barrel-vaulted cellar (see *below*) and served it from a half-sash window in the hallway (see *above*). A bottle, marked "W E Burrows of Derby, 1872", was found under one of the thrawls.

The former public house was then divided in two, and its side entry converted to make a second front door leading to a fourth staircase.

Thrawl in the barrel-vaulted cellar

Former Men's Reading Room. Now the Music Room.

Upstairs the main assembly room (32'x17'), together with a downstairs room (14'x14') with a small kitchen, became the Men's Reading Room (subscription 1 penny a week). This was rented at £4 per annum and run by a Reading Room Committee.

It had a piano and provided the rehearsal rooms for a local minstrel group of fiddles and banjos, who gave performances in the Parish (now Village) Hall. The Reading Room Secretary also looked after the Library in the Wesleyan Chapel (see Chapter 15). For my part the main Reading Room provides an ideal location for six keyboard instruments and the core of a library of some 12,000 books.

Whist drives were held here in the 1920s and the whole property (House, Reading Rooms, Coach House and two acres) was sold by auction for £525 on 10th March, 1931. (See Chapter 28: The "Great Sale" of 1931). For a time the Richardson family, who acquired the house, kept the old Reading Rooms running as a village facility. The Toc H Club (an all-male gathering) rented the house in 1932 - Frank Stone's brother, Walter, being the pre-World War 2 secretary and Frank himself secretary post-War. During the War servicemen were entertained to tea and it was also an ARP (Air Raid Precaution) Centre. Later Quarndon WI used it for meetings.

For over 30 years, following the War, the Quarndon Amateur Dramatic Society used the house for rehearsals. When we moved in we found a box of old costumes and curtains, together with programmes for the 1979 production of The Sound of Murder (see Chapter 25) and a list of 61 previous productions. The Society had put a label on the front door to identify the place as "The Quandary".

Derbyshire Record Office: D2375/5/6 & 11 Courtesy: County & Diocesan Archivist.

QUARNDON HALL
FRONT ENTRANCE
AFTER THE FIRE 15 OCT 1904

Quarndon Hall
Before and after the fire.

17. Quarndon Hall

THIS house, with its alternating shades of brick courses, was built in 1841 at a cost of what is said to have been around £3,000. It is situated behind a high wall halfway down Church Road on the left and is not open to the public. According to the local historian, Roy Christian (writing in *Derbyshire Life & Countryside*, in June, 1966), the land on which it was built was probably sold by the third Lord Scarsdale - "a bachelor who found the cost of living in the inflationary period that followed the Napoleonic Wars so extortionate that he was obliged to leave *Kedleston Hall* for *Farnah Hall* (a smaller house on the estate), sack 30 servants and sell some building land out of sight of the windows of Kedleston". The purchaser was Dorothy Wilmot-Sitwell, an unmarried descendant of the Sitwell family. She called the house *Quarndon Cottage* and lived there with her sister, Selina. On their death the house was left to their niece, Harriet, who was married to the Hon. William Monk Jervis (1827-1909). He was a barrister, Justice of the Peace and president of Derbyshire County Cricket Club. He enlarged the house and re-named it *Quarndon Hall*.

But, during the early hours of Saturday, 15th October, 1904, the *Hall* suffered "a disastrous fire". The *Derbyshire Advertiser's* report of the drama provides a fascinating insight into life in a medium-sized country estate at the beginning of the 20th century:

> "The family retired to rest shortly before 11 o'clock on Friday night, and at that time everything appeared to be safe and sound. The inmates consisted of Mr and Mrs Jervis and seven servants...It was shortly after three o'clock that the discovery was first made by Mrs Jervis. She states that she smelt smoke in the bedroom...and opened the bedroom door, when she saw the landing was full of dense smoke. She realised at once that the house was on fire, but, with a presence of mind upon which she cannot be too warmly complimented, she rang the bells for her maid and prepared to assist her husband to make a hurried departure. Mr Jervis, we may explain, is in his 78th year, and not so active as he formerly was; indeed, he has for some months past been unable to get about without leaning on the arm of his valet."

"Mrs Jervis," the report goes on, "with great devotion, thought only of her husband and his means of escape." They eventually, "clad only in their night clothes and dressing-gown, left the burning building by a side door, and passed through the conservatory into the garden."

So what of the seven servants?

> "Arden, the butler, roused Wyatt, one of the gardeners, and, between them, they managed to reach the maidservants on the second floor at the back of the house by ladder. But Mary Kirk and Annie Walwark - two maids at the front of the house - had no time to wait for the ladder.

> They tied the sheets of their bed together, fastened them to the bedstead and let themselves out the window...Miss Kirk's descent was safely made, but Miss Walwark hurt herself in the fall, not seriously, but sufficient to cause her to faint...Mr Hampshire, the landlord of *The Joiner's Arms*, was called upon to supply some brandy, Mr Jervis's stock being quite unobtainable. Miss Walwark, however, soon recovered and her condition was attributed largely to the excitement of the occasion."

The method by which the Fire Brigade was alerted also makes interesting reading:

"One of the first things that was done after the fire was discovered was to despatch one of the gardeners to Derby on a bicycle to give the alarm; the postmistress was also knocked up and easily persuaded to send a telegram to the Derby Fire Brigade. This latter alternative proved the most expeditious; and one of the Corporation fire engines...was on its way to Quarndon at full speed before the cyclist messenger had reached his destination."

The paper reports that the interior of the *Hall* and its contents were almost all destroyed (although "Mr Jervis's butler had the good fortune to recover a sum of £60 in gold, which was in his room at the time of the fire.")

The *Hall* was totally restored and re-occupied by the Jervises 18 months later.

The interior of the *Hall* has all the principal rooms leading off a central hall and staircase.

William Jervis added Canadian pine panelling to the library (later a nursery, now a sitting room) and drawing room - the latter having been extended by the addition of a spacious, south-facing bay. Both rooms have stone fireplaces with wooden mantelpieces - as does the large dining room. A huge conservatory at right angles to the house was destroyed in the 1904 fire, but was replaced towards the end of the 20th century.

On Jervis's death the house reverted to the Sitwell family and was sold in 1926 to Mary, Lady FitzHerbert, widow of the 5th baronet. A later occupant was her son, the Venerable Henry FitzHerbert, Archdeacon of Derby, 1943-52, and his wife, Margaret. In 1950, they exchanged houses with Arthur and Gina Richardson of *The Old Vicarage*. (Arthur Richardson captained Derbyshire to the County Cricket Championship in 1936 - see Chapter 23.)

The Folly - "forming an excellent focal point for the whole garden".
(Painting by a local artist, courtesy Nancy Bird.)

The Pond - "from where an immaculately maintained lawn climbs to the *Hall*".

In 1979 the *Hall* was bought by Paul and Nancy Bird, of Birds (Derby) Limited, confectioners & pastrycooks. According to Frank Constable, former Parks Superintendent, Derby City Council, writing in *Derbyshire Life & Countryside* in July, 1996: "Mr and Mrs Bird and their gardener, Mr Peter Fields, created a garden to compete with the best in the Midlands. Their enthusiasm took them to all quarters of the British Isles in their quest for plants - acquiring one thousand varieties of rhododendron, eighty of camellia and thirteen hundred heathers."

Frank Constable

The area includes a two-acre woodland garden ("created on ground sloping to a pond, from where an immaculately maintained lawn climbs to the *Hall*"). There's also a rock garden, involving 100 tons of stone ("in which a sparkling cascade of water was introduced to feed into the pond"). Framing the rock garden is a folly ("with six pillars...which originally had provided a centre-piece to one of the hundred or so themed gardens at the Stoke Garden Festival...forming an excellent focal point for the whole garden"). The former tennis court has been transformed into a formal Italian garden; there's also a secret garden ("for all seasons") and a quiet garden.

Paul Bird died in 1992, but Nancy continues to care for the seven-acre garden, with the capable help of her head gardener, Lucien Emmerson. Prior to 2008 the garden was the venue for the annual Church Fête in June and for the occasional concert.

Courtesy: Raymonds Press Agency

In 1964, the Church Fête, held in the grounds of *Quarndon Hall,* was opened by the Ticknall farmer and TV & radio personality, Ted Moult (*left*).

Photo: Liz Harris

The Fête in 2007

18. Other interesting houses

SEVERAL appeals have been made through the *Quarndon Parish Council Newsletter* for villagers to provide the *Quarndon: Then & Now* Team with details of, and stories about, any houses of particular historic interest in Quarndon. In addition to information included in the two foregoing chapters, responses have been forthcoming about the following:

Quarndon Hill

***Quarndon Hill*: from the garden**

 This house on The Common is shown on a 1760 map as *Hill Cottage*. It was built partly of stone at the bottom and Quarndon brick at the top. It consisted of one large room with an arched passage leading to a kitchen with cellar. There was also a groom's cottage and a gardener's cottage (now No. 74 The Common).

In 1905 the house was greatly extended in Butterley Engineering brick. When it was bought by Hadden & Mary Richardson in 1934, it had been empty for 10 years. (Hadden Richardson, who died in 1968, was senior partner of the firm of W & J Richardson, tanners, of Eagle Leather Works, Derby, which dated back to the 18th century.) They pulled down the old kitchen, scullery, staircase and five maids' bedrooms and built a Badminton Hall, which is currently used by numerous groups. When they moved in they took over a large greenhouse and heated frames in which tomatoes, cucumbers, French beans and peas were grown in time for Christmas.

Their son, James, recalls: "I was told that the lawns were mown with a pony with large leather pads on its feet. The water supply came from a spring and was pumped up the hill, using a 3-manpower gas engine. After all the partying in the 1936-9 period - with tennis on the grass court, croquet and bowls on the front lawn and badminton in the Hall - the outbreak of War must have come as a cultural shock! Two gardeners were called up and the four maids left for the war effort. There wasn't enough fuel to heat the whole house so we lived in two rooms downstairs with very little heating upstairs. After the War my parents demolished the servants' sitting room, the pantry and the silver room. The cook retired and my mother took over her duties. In 1955 my sister, Judith, started the Quarn Hill Riding School."

Fern Hill

***Fern Hill*: from the Lake**

This house, behind *Quarndon House* on The Common, overlooks a sunken lake. It is the home of James (see *previous page*) & Sue Richardson. James writes:

"When I was nine years old I remember my parents talking about Boden's Lace and what a shame it was that the Mill in Derby had closed in the 1930s. During that decade the Bodens moved from *The Friary* in Derby (now *The Friary Hotel*) to *Fern Hill*. My parents went on to relate how Mr Boden used to sit in his bedroom shooting rabbits through the window and sending his dog to collect them. They also said that the garden was a jungle and that there was once a large lake there with a flat-bottomed boat floating on it.

I found this intriguing and decided to explore it with Billy, our spaniel. We walked across the fields and came to a small wood, which was impregnable. Beyond, I could just make out a small pool of water with, yes, part of a boat, but I couldn't see the house. I decided that it was impossible to explore further. Little did I know that, 15 years later, I would buy *Fern Hill* and embark on 'The lost gardens of *Fern Hill*!'"

Brook Cottage

This former Toll House (see Chapter 7: *Boundaries, roads & turnpikes*) was built of brick with a slate-tiled roof. The garden slopes down to a stream running from the site of Quarndon's former Mill (see Chapter 3) to the Markeaton Brook.

It was bought at auction on 27th April, 1975, by Ian Aitken, who carried out major renovations and refurbishments to the property. These included insulating the roof, rendering the outside walls (a District Council requirement - against Ian's wishes!), replacing the floors and staircase, renewing windows and defective brickwork, rewiring, major plumbing alterations and installing a damp course.

Our pictures show the cottage before and after refurbishment.

Photo: David Widdows

Toll House windows: then & now

Park Nook

Aerial view before alterations

Map of Park Nook (Early 20th century)

Source unknown

Courtesy: Curzon Papers, Kedleston Hall.

This group of buildings - with *Park Nook Farm* to its north (see page 43) - fills the corner enclosed by the top of Inn Lane and its 'hairpin' junction with The Common. It was originally known as Baker's Green and was the property of the Kedleston Estate until it was sold in 1961.

It comprises four dwellings. In the centre are the former *Kedleston Estate Offices* (recently re-named *Park Nook Grange*); south of this is an extended house (formerly *The Victorian House*, but now divided into *The Georgian House* to the west and *Park Nook House* to the east), and to the north (on The Common) is *Park Nook Cottage*.

The oldest property is *The Georgian House* - a former farmhouse, built in about 1750. This was extended eastwards in 1873. According to invoices from Charles Hampshire (of the workshops in the grounds of the *Joiners' Arms*), the total cost of building the extension was nearly £900.

The Victorian House was for many years the official residence of the Kedleston Estate Manager, who worked at the neighbouring offices.

Park Nook Grange - an L-shaped, gabled house - was probably built at the end of the 18th century. When it was extended in 1983 its listed chimneys were preserved. Inside is what Maxwell Craven describes as "an excellent quality turned stick baluster staircase with curving rail - very much in the Regency tradition". The late Ursula Eddowes, who spent her childhood and 'teens at *The Victorian House*, said: "We rented the whole of Park Nook. The Estate Office" [*Park Nook Grange*] "had a very nice staircase and two upstairs rooms - one my brother used as his radio room and the other we used for all sorts of things. It was a gymnasium at one time. My father kept all his gardening tools downstairs - it was sacrilege really!"

Park Nook Grange

Park Nook Cottage

Park Nook Cottage is Victorian. The *Georgian House* has a square, four-windowed Georgian frontage, with added porch.

Park Nook House, which has a red brick Georgian double-storey bay with Victorian extension, is the home of Bryan and Liz Harris. Liz writes:

"We discovered the house in 1983 when we'd just moved to Derbyshire. It had already been separated from *The Georgian House* and then left abandoned for over two years. A chimney pot had fallen through the roof, the hall tiles had disappeared and there were no floor boards in the main bedroom. The front door and some of the windows had been left open and Sunday afternoon 'visitors' had helped themselves to door knobs, escutcheons and general fittings on their way through. Mould was gathering on the walls, cornices were parting company with the ceilings, there was no electricity, gas or plumbing and no kitchen, bathroom or loo! It did, however, have the most stunning views and, with three months' building work and the help of friends, we were able to make it habitable."

The Georgian House

Park Nook House

Quarndon House

Quarndon House: **front entrance**

Built in the 1870s, this was originally called *The Knoll* and owned by Thomas Crump, Chairman of Thomas Crump & Company, Plumbers' Merchants, Friargate, Derby.

In 1911 it was sold to Harriet, widow of the Hon. William Monk Jervis, of *Quarndon Hall*, barrister, who had died in 1909 (see Chapter 17). The same year Henry Royce was a tenant there (see Chapter 27). In 1921, it came into the possession of the Ann family of the Midland Drapery Company. (See also Chapter 29.)

In 1991 it was sold to Don & Pauline Prime. (Don is the founder-owner of Prime Constructions, Aston-on-Trent. He also chaired the *Magic Cancer* Appeal, which raised £1.25 million for equipment for Derby hospitals.) They discovered that, in its pre-War heyday, the house had employed a staff of 10 and, with the installation of underground heating in the greenhouses, had grown out-of-season vegetables. As is illustrated on the *opposite page*, they demolished the seven-bedroom servants' quarters on the north side of the house and extended the drawing room on the south side. They also remodelled the kitchen, which had once been a ballroom.

Quarndon House: from the garden. (Drawing room extension on *left*.)

Demolishing the Servants' Wing

The site today

163 & 165 Burley Lane

Photo: David Widdows

Sunny Hill & Sunnyside, 163 & 165 Burley Lane

Alan West (of No. 163) writes: "These semi-detached houses - called *Sunny Hill* and *Sunnyside* - were built in 1892 on the site of a decaying property that had been demolished. They belonged to the Kedleston Estate and were originally intended for staff occupation - the butler in *Sunny Hill* and the assistant butler in *Sunnyside*. Some readers may remember that, before Sulley's Field was built on the other side of Burley Lane, a pump on the site - erected over a spring - existed near to the road. Apparently, pre-1892, water from this spring, draining under the road, was directed into a man-made channel, stretching the width of the gardens of numbers 163 and 165. This was used for fattening trout. Water from the spring still passes underground to the field below, causing bogging problems."

As is featured in Chapter 28, in 1931 the "Great Sale" of many Kedleston Estate properties took place. The sale catalogue lists *Sunny Hill* as containing: Porch, sitting room, kitchen, scullery with copper & sink (pump over), 2 cellars, 3 bedrooms, outside coalhouse, pail closet and large garden. *Sunnyside* is listed as having similar accommodation to *Sunny Hill* and again a large garden.

Post-World War I houses

David Widdows writes: "Following the 'Great Sale' of 1931, which made new areas of land available for development, nearly all the houses on Burley Lane and Burley Drive were built during the seven years before the outbreak of World War 2. There were two architects who shared the design work, independent of each other: Peter Woore, who worked on his own, and Bernard Widdows (my father) of Naylor, Sale & Widdows. So similar are the styles of these two architects that it's difficult to determine which of them designed what on Burley Lane. However, it's known that all the houses on Burley Drive, built during that time, were the work of Bernard Widdows. In 1935 he designed *St Paul's Vicarage* (No. 149 Church Road) and, in 1937, his own house - opposite the Woodlands Lane Water Tower."

St Paul's Vicarage (1935). Designed by Bernard Widdows.

Photo: John Fallon

▲
▼
The Barn, 93 Burley Lane (with commanding views across Allestree Park),
which Peter Woore designed for himself in 1963.

Photo: John Fallon

Photo: David Widdows

St Paul's Church
Through the Lantern Arch

19. St Paul's Church

*(The Editor is indebted to the **Rev'd WILLIAM BATES** for his assistance with this Chapter and Chapter 2. Additional information for both Chapters: G J Charles Cox: Notes on the Churches of Derbyshire, Vol. 4, Edmunds/Bemrose, 1968, & Charles James Payne: Derbyshire Churches Old & New, Moray Press, 1893.)*

St Paul's Church from the South West

St Paul's Church from the East

BY 1871, the population of Quarndon having risen to over 550, the main development of the village was taking place at its centre - no longer in the vicinity of the Chapel, Mill and former *Old Quarndon Hall*, but up the hill on the present **Church Road**. Consequently, land on top of the hill - together with a contribution of £1,000 - was donated for a new **St Paul's Church** by the Rev'd Alfred Curzon, 4th Baron Scarsdale (see page 96). The total cost of the building was just over £4,000, of which the villagers raised over £2,000 and their "neighbours and friends" £1,000.

The Grade II-listed Church has a two-storey **South West Tower**, surmounted by a **Spire**, with four **Dormer Windows** and **Spire Lights** near the top.

It was designed by the architectural partnership, Giles & Brookhouse of Derby (fee: £195) and built by the Derby firm of Edwin Thomson for £3,470 (plus nearly £600 for sub-contractors, materials, etc). The foundation stone was laid by the then Lady Scarsdale on 5th November, 1872, and the building was consecrated by George Selwyn, Bishop of Lichfield, on 16th April, 1874. (In case the name sounds familiar, Selwyn had rowed for Cambridge in the first University Boat Race in 1829 and had been the first Bishop of New Zealand & Melanesia from 1841 to 1867. Selwyn College, Cambridge, was founded in his memory.)

In the late 1890s a lively church community was said to have developed, with "a Choir consisting of two or three ladies, a similar number of boys and three or four male adults, who chant and hymn in such a tasteful, delicate and harmonious manner as would give points to many a town choir". It is also on record that, attached to the Church, were "lady district visitors, a reading room, a Girls' Friendly Society, a Bible class and mothers' meetings". (As William Bates observes: "The 'reading room' - as an alternative to the pub? - suggests a concern for temperance.")

If you're interested in Victorian church architecture, or you would simply like to find out more about your parish church, the details are as follows - each major feature printed, with initial capitals, in **Bold**.

Nikolaus Pevsner, in the Derbyshire edition of his Penguin Books series, *The Buildings of England*, describes St Paul's as "tasteless and restless, rock-faced, with SW broach-spire" (though William Bates thinks "tasteless and restless" may refer to the interior, following alterations carried out in the 1930s).

On the four corners at the base of the **Spire** are **Carved Heads** representing the four Evangelists. They are: the Man (Matthew): south-west corner; the Lion (Mark): north-west corner; the Ox (Luke): north-east corner; and the Eagle (John): south-east corner.

Photos: David Widdows

| **St Matthew** | **St Mark** | **St Luke** | **St John** |

In 1897, to mark Queen Victoria's Diamond Jubilee, a **Striking Clock**, with a 5ft diameter cast iron skeleton dial, was installed in the Tower by John Smith & Sons of Derby for £72 - the **Bell** being cast from the two bells taken from the old Chapel by John Taylor & Co. of Loughborough. It weighs 7cwt 1qtr 4lb and has a mouth diameter of 2ft 9.25 inches.

The **Clock Workings** are enclosed in a cupboard (to protect them from stone dust and bird lime) and have been maintained by Smiths ever since. On the walls of the cupboard are listed the names of numerous Quarndon villagers since 1897.

Photo: Liz Harris

Photo: Nicholas Smith

The skeleton clock   **Clock workings**

The clock was converted to automatic winding in 1984 and, according to Nicholas Smith of Coach Drive, Quarndon (Chairman of Smith of Derby Group, Ltd, and fourth generation of the family firm), "it was fitted with a pendulum regulator in 2003 and upgraded to global positioning accuracy in 2004".

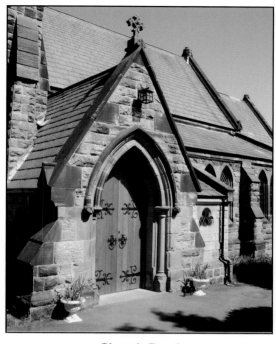

Church Porch

Vicar's Vestry Door

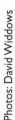

Photos: David Widdows

Adjacent to the **Porch** is a **WC for the Disabled** - given anonymously by a parishioner who died in 2006.

Because the ground falls away so steeply south-east of the Church, the **Chancel** is heavily buttressed and the outer door of the **Vicar's Vestry** (which is at internal floor level) is reached by a flight of steps. **The Crypt**, with access from outside, is at ground level.

According to Maurice Oakley: "In around 1936 Charlie Slack, the Church Verger, of *Fields Farm*, committed suicide in the boiler room under the Church. I saw them carry his body out on a stretcher. He was an elderly man and it was said that he'd been wrongly accused of being over-familiar with a woman he'd found blackberrying at the farm. The accusation had played on his mind."

Ground level Boiler Room & Crypt

SE Buttress

Photos: David Widdows

East Window

The **East Window** of St Paul's illustrates (appropriately) the Conversion of Saul of Tarsus - later known as Paul - struck down by a shaft of light from Heaven on the road to Damascus. (The city of Damascus can be seen in the background.) The scroll in the top light reads: "Saul, why persecutest thou me?" (*Acts of the Apostles*, 9:4) and the inscription at the bottom reads: "To the glory of God. A thank offering, 1896." It was donated by Joseph Cadman, who had left Quarndon as a young man in clogs to seek his fortune and went on to found the Star Tea Company.

Photo: David Widdows

The Altar

The **Altar** is inscribed: "In thanksgiving to God for the parenthood of Henry Edward and Margaret Elinor FitzHerbert, this altar table was given in 1960 by their seven children." (The grave of Henry FitzHerbert, Archdeacon of Derby from 1943-52, and his wife, is on the left as you approach the Church Porch.)

The **Altar Frontal** in the above photograph is by the late Ursula Eddowes - a founder member of the Quarndon Ladies' Guild, who look after the church brasses and altar linen. (See Chapter 13.)

The oak **Altar Rails** were donated in 1931 in memory of Canon Francis John Adams, who lived at *Selworthy* on Burley Lane. He was the first Secretary of the Derby Diocese when it was created in 1927. (See also St John's Chapel, later in this chapter.)

The **Choir Stalls** were dedicated in 1929 as "a thank offering for the safe return of the men of Quarndon who served in the Great War, 1914-1918". (The inscription is illustrated in Chapter 26: *Quarndon in Wartime: The Home Front & "foreign field"*, along with pictures of the Memorials to those killed in World Wars 1 and 2 on the Nave North Aisle Wall and by the West Wall of the Churchyard.)

The **Choir Panelling** and **Vestry Screen** were installed "to commemorate the safe return of men and women from the Second World War".

Photo: David Widdows

When you enter the Church, note that the walls on either side of the huge **Chancel Arch** are not of equal width!

North corbel

Photos: David Widdows

South corbel

The Arch is supported on each side by three **Dwarfed Columns**, supported by a **Carved Corbel** depicting a praying angel.

136

The Brass Lectern

Organ, Lectern, Vestry Screen & Choir Stalls

Photos: David Widdows

The **Brass Lectern** cost £85 10s - £32 10s of which was collected by local children over an 8-year period. It was first used on Christmas Day, 1920.

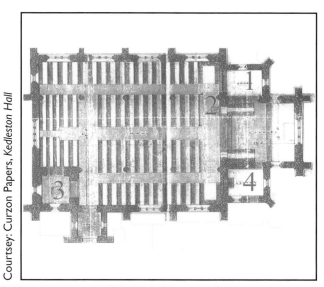

Courtsey: Curzon Papers, *Kedleston Hall*

Original Church plan

The Organ - as can be seen on the plan *left* - was originally in the alcove to the right of its present position (now the Choir Vestry). It was relocated in 1920. According to Rodney Tomkins (*Pipe Organs in Churches & Chapels of the Derbyshire East Derwent & Ecclesbourne Valley,* publ. Scarthin Books, 1995): "The organ is by J M Grunwell of Derby and almost certainly dates from the building of the present church, though some of the pipes (and perhaps even the console, with its tall, vertical column of drawstops) may be of earlier vintage". A plaque on the Organ states: "The electric lighting was installed in this Church in 1947 and the organ casing was fixed in 1949. They were the gifts of Oswald Josiah Jackson of *The Grange*, Quarndon." Alterations to the Organ took place in 1971 and it was overhauled in 1991. The original positioning was: 1. Organ (now Choir Vestry); 2. Pulpit; 3. Font; 4. Vicar's Vestry (as now).

The Pulpit

Photo: David Widdows

The **Pulpit** is a memorial to Ann, wife of Henry Cheetham, Vicar of Quarndon, 1858-71, who became Bishop of Sierra Leone. (It originally stood on the north side of the aisle, but was moved when the organ was relocated.) The Pulpit Pedestal has recently been lowered to create a better rapport between the preacher and the congregation.

The **Nave** has a **Vaulted Pine Roof** and lean-to **Aisles**. There are four pointed-arched **Bays** on the north side and three on the south, with a smaller arch to the west. The **Arches**, which consist of stone blocks in alternating colours, are supported by round **Pillars**. The **Floor Tiles** are in red, grey and yellow.

A distinctive feature of the **Side Aisle Windows** is the use of free-standing **Pillarettes** to divide the lights, thus forming two **Triple Arcades** in the South Aisle, three in the North Aisle (one of which is now obscured by the organ) and one **Double Arcade** in the **Children's** (NW) **Corner.**

The **Furniture** in the Children's Corner was a gift in 1962 from Ida Walkerdine, in memory of her husband. It has recently been fitted with child-proof gates.

Nave & Chancel from NW

Photo: David Widdows

The South Nave Aisle forms **St John's Chapel**, which was dedicated in 1931. An inscription on the Altar Cross reads: "This side chapel was dedicated in loving and grateful thanks for the life of Francis John Adams, Canon of Southwell and later of Derby." (See page 135.) The **Sanctuary Rails** were provided by Hedley & Sylvia Richardson in 1962 in memory of their children, Diana (7) and Anthony (15). The Chapel also contains a **Reading Desk** (1982), in memory of Richard Anthony Hook (17) and the **Prayer Stall** (1989) commemorates the Rev'd Arthur Noble, who ministered as a retired priest at St Paul's during the 1980s.

In the Chapel are two **Stained Glass Windows**.

From *left* to *right*: the one at the east end, in memory of the same Canon Adams and his wife, Mary, depicts St John, Apostle & Evangelist.

The next carries two quotations from St Paul: "I have fought the good fight" (*II Timothy*, 4:7) and "By the grace of God, I am what I am."(*I Corinthians*, 15:10).

The one at the west end (under the bell tower) depicts the young Jesus with a scroll and carries the inscription: "The grace of God was upon him" (*Luke*, 2:40). It was provided by the children of the village through a series of fundraising efforts in 1933.

Photo: David Widdows

St John's Chapel

Photos: David Widdows

Photo: Liz Harris

Stained glass windows, south wall

139

The Font

Photo: David Widdows

The Derbyshire spar **Font** originally stood under the bell tower (see plan on page 137), but, in 1969, it was moved to its present position at the west end of the Nave - thus allowing more space for larger baptism parties.

The **Sound System** was installed in memory of John Robotham (of Woodlands Lane), senior partner, Robotham & Co, solicitors, and the **Hearing Loop** is in memory of Paul Bird (of *Quarndon Hall*), chairman & managing director of Birds (Derby) Limited, confectioners & pastrycooks.

The Church was built to accommodate a congregation of 366, but, because of the relocation of the Organ and Font and the creation of St John's Chapel, this is now 210. From 1995 to 2007, average Sunday attendance declined from 89 to 55. At the time of publication, the population of the Anglican parish is 1,832, with 82 on the Church Electoral Roll. The Parochial Church Council consists of nine members, plus the Vicar (Chairman), the Curate, the Reader and the two Churchwardens.

The parish is in the Rural Deanery of Duffield, the Archdeaconry of Derby, the Diocese of Derby and the Province of Canterbury.

In the year 2000, as part of the village Millennium Celebrations & Commemorations (see Chapter 32), the **Church Weathervane** was re-gilded. While this work was in progress, the steeplejack identified £18,000 worth of essential repairs to the top of the Spire. A successful appeal was launched to cover this and other restoration work to the Church and Village Hall.

The Rev'd William Bates

The current **Priest-in-Charge** of St Paul's, Quarndon, **the Rev'd William Bates**, who is also Vicar of St Nicholas, Allestree, writes:

"Quarndon's Victorian clergy were men of conviction who, according to the best practice of their time, provided much of the structure for the life of St Paul's today. Older members of 21st century St Paul's have fond memories of Alan Andrews and Arthur Milroy. A recent e-mail from John Morison reflected on the healthy social life and generous care shown by church families during his time as vicar (1986-99). In 2008 some of those same people are frail, or have died, and the life of the church is taking a new course.

If change can be relied on as one of life's constants, one value that remains the same is the close relationship between the Church and the Primary School. This is currently reflected in the School's participation in All Age services and in a weekly telling of Bible stories by an *Open the Book* team. St Paul's vision statement stresses the importance of ministry among younger people and money has been given to enable the employment of a children and family worker in conjunction with St Nick's, Allestree. Other aspects of the Church's vision include outreach through *Alpha Courses* ("discussing questions about the meaning of life"), spiritually nourishing worship and growth in care among older people. All this and more is attempted in the belief that God calls his Church to invite everyone into the experience of his love and goodness and glory - an experience given by the Holy Spirit to all who open themselves, in faith, to the risen Christ."

Incumbents since Quarndon became a parish are as follows:

Sep, 1762 - Sep, 1802:	Thomas Manlove, MA
Sep, 1802 - Jul, 1858:	William Barber
Jul, 1858 - Feb, 1871:	Henry Cheetham, BA (Later Bishop of Sierra Leone)
Feb, 1871 - Aug, 1910:	William George Nourse
Jan, 1911 - Dec, 1915:	Martin Trietschel, MA (A German surname, later changed to Trevor)
Feb, 1916 - Aug, 1921:	Thomas Vyner Southey
Sep, 1921 - Mar, 1925:	James Robinson, MA
Mar, 1925 - Jul, 1928:	Frederick Franklin Watson
Sep, 1928 - Mar, 1930:	John Henry Bell Hammond
Aug, 1930 - Aug, 1934:	Alan Walter Grudgington, BA
May, 1935 - Jul, 1958:	Emmerson Richardson
Oct, 1958 - Jul, 1979:	Alan Robert Williams Andrews, AKC
Aug, 1979 - Sep, 1985:	Arthur Rundle Milroy, MA
May, 1986 - Sep, 1999:	John Donald Morison, ALCD
Apr, 2000 -	William Frederic Bates, MA

The **Churchyard Gates** (since renewed) are inscribed: "To the glory of God and in memory of Frank Ernest & Mary Pullon, by their sons, 1960."

Woodlands Lane Water Tower

20. Quarndon's water supply

By JOHN BANHAM & OTHERS

IN the 1800s the Kedleston Estate took on a significant role in establishing a water supply system to Quarndon. An hydraulic ram pump was installed at the exit to a spring in the valley between Church Road and *The Kedleston Hotel*. This delivered water through a pipe into tanks under what was *Montpelier Farm* (on the top side of Montpelier). From these tanks pipes were laid into the village. However, most houses and cottages were without running water, having to rely on standpipes in the streets or wells in their gardens.

There are no standpipes in Quarndon now, but our picture shows an example of one still in existence in the village of Ticknall.

Ticknall standpipe

Photo: Don Hall

Subsequently, the Estate laid more pipes from springs in the village - one of them under what is now Sulley's Field. Frank Stone recalls that, as a boy, he and his friends "used to lift the manhole cover at the top of Sulley's Field, stick our heads down and listen to the rams pumping water into the underground reservoirs!"

The late Ivan Cope said: "You could draw water from an artesian well at *Sycamore Cottage* by *Holly Bank Farm*."

Later, a network of pipes was laid, bringing water to some of the larger houses. But, as David Widdows points out, Mrs Stone - Frank's mother - was drawing water from a well at the front of her house, 99 Church Road, until the winter of 1962/3, when the pump froze and the handle came off! (See right.)

Mrs Stone's broken pump

A significant development in the village water supply took place after the passing of the Derby Corporation Act of 1927. This gave the town powers to extend the Corporation's supply to include the parish of Quarndon and improve the quality of the water provided.

In 1932 the reinforced concrete Water Tower was built in Woodlands Lane, receiving its water from a pumping station in Allestree Park. This, in turn, was supplied from a large trunk main which transferred water from Drum Hill Reservoir, Little Eaton, to the south and west sides of Derby. At the same time new water mains were laid in Woodlands Lane, Burley Lane and Church Road.

Photo: Don Hall

Horse trough, *Holly Bank,* Church Road

According to Clifford Aldwinckle, of Montpelier, the Water Tower was built by F C Construction, Ltd, of Derby, under the direction of Bill Henderson, a Tynesider, who later supervised the post-War reconstruction of the Consett Steel Works in Co. Durham.

The water supply to The Common came from an underground source at a borehole in Belper, via Farnah Green Reservoir, and this system - the responsibility of the then Belper Rural District Council - was connected to the Derby Corporation supply at Cumberhills Road.

A closed sluice valve at the junction of The Common and Church Road isolated the two systems. A horse trough in the wall of *Holly Bank,* No. 88 Church Road (see *above*), was fed from a spring.

Quarndon's water from the Tower system came from three sources: Derwent Valley Reservoirs (soft moorland water); Homesford Cottage (hard limestone water from underground), and Little Eaton (medium hardness from the River Derwent). These were mixed at Drum Hill, producing a supply of medium hardness to the Tower. The separate water supply to The Common was hard.

The responsibility for water supplies changed in 1965 when the South Derbyshire Water Board came into being, providing water supplies to the southern part of the county. It was formed by the Derby Corporation Water Department, which already supplied water into Quarndon, then extended west to Ashbourne, north to Matlock and east to Ilkeston. To the south of Derby, water was already supplied by the South Staffordshire Water Company.

Then, after 1974, when the Severn Trent Water Authority was formed, water for most of Derbyshire was administered by the Derwent Division, based at Raynesway in Derby.

During the Authority's period of administration, the borehole at Belper was taken out of service, the water supplied to Farnah Green Reservoir became a mixture of Derwent Valley Reservoirs and Homesford Cottage underground water and the Woodlands Lane Water Tower was taken out of service.

The next change to take place was in 1989 when the water industry in England and Wales was privatised. Since then Severn Trent plc has spent large sums of money refurbishing the water treatment plant at Bamford (which receives raw water from the Derwent Valley Reservoirs) and the one at Little Eaton (receiving raw water from the River Derwent). Currently the top of the Water Tower is festooned with a number of microwave dishes belonging to several telecommunications operators.

(John Banham was Operations Manager, Derwent Division, Severn Trent Water Authority, from 1975 to 1985.)

21. Electricity comes to Quarndon

By JAMES RICHARDSON

IN 1893 Derby Corporation built Full Street Electric Light Station on the bank of the River Derwent and installed 70 arc street lights in Derby. The site was chosen because of (a) the large quantities of water needed to cool the condensers and (b) its proximity to St Mary's Wharf, where coal from Denby mine could be brought, via Little Eaton, and conveyed from the wharf by horse and cart - later by lorry - to the power station. By 1898 the Corporation was generating at 2000 volts and transforming it down to either 100 or 200 volts. This enabled them to supply electricity to about 400 Derby homes. By 1912 a 4000-volt transmission cable (mainly overhead) reached Quarndon, terminating at *Vine Cottage* on Church Road, where it was transformed down to 200/210 volts. The transformer was known as a "Bobby's Hat" because its top resembled a policeman's helmet!

© NE Midland Photographic Record. All rights reserved.

"Bobby's Hat" transformer, *Vine Cottage*

The transformer today

In 1915 a "real live" showroom and demonstration kitchen was opened in London Road, Derby (later in Irongate) and these were becoming great centres of attraction in the town.

From this humble beginning they promoted the electric cooker, electric fire and, later, toasters, vacuum cleaners and even food mixers.

Pole-mounted transformers (reducing the incoming electricity supply from 11,000 to 240 volts)

Snowdrop Cottage

Cricket Club

Senior Citizens' Bungalows

By 1952 Full Street was supplying power to the National Grid. Subsequently it was decided to standardise the domestic supply to 240 volts. An 11000-volt 3-phase overhead cable was installed from Duffield to behind *Snowdrop Cottage* on The Common, then on to *Vine Cottage*, with branches off at the Cricket Ground and the Senior Citizens' Bungalows. This was transformed down to 240 volts and new cables were laid throughout the village. (Prior to this, all domestic appliances had to be either replaced or converted to take the higher voltage.) Woodlands Lane, Montpelier and Burley Lane are supplied from two transformers on Burley Lane.

I remember Barry Topliff, who lived at No. 3 The Common and worked for the Electricity Board. He was in charge of a gang of about 20 men who dug trenches and laid the electric cables. The first few men would lead the team, digging down about 9 inches, to be followed behind with other men taking the soil out to 18, then 24 inches. The remaining men would lay the big cable in the trench and fill it in. It was surprising how far they could proceed in a day! (Our picture shows the same work being carried out by a previous generation!)

Courtesy: The Joiners' Arms

Laying the electricity cable outside *The Joiners' Arms*, 1912

22. Street lighting

By COLIN RAYBOULD & JAMES RICHARDSON

TODAY street lighting in Quarndon is taken very much for granted, but its history is a very chequered one.

Gas street-lamp

Photo: *Derby Evening Telegraph*

Former electric street-lamp

In 1866, a gas supply was laid from Duffield to Quarndon. It came from a gasworks built by a member of the Hampshire family, whose workshops were at *The Joiners' Arms*. (See Chapter 12.)

The first section of gas street lighting was installed in 1914, supplied by the Derby Gas Light & Coke Company, Ltd, and funded by subscription from the larger houses in the village. It continued in use until 1915, when it was turned off for the duration of World War I.

The initial installation consisted of fifteen gaslights on cast iron standards, strategically placed at intervals of 150 to 190 yards from the bottom of Church Road and along The Common to *Snowdrop Cottage*. Responsibility for the installation and maintenance of the system lay in the hands of an appointed body known as the 'Gas Lighting Committee' (part of the Derby Gas Light & Coke Co.). But in 1915, following the restrictions imposed by wartime conditions, the Committee ceased to exist and was never reconvened. So, effectively, the street-lighting system belonged to no-one!

(Parish Council concerns regarding the possibility of street lights becoming 'pathfinders' for Zeppelins is covered in Chapter 26.)

In 1937 the Parish Council assumed ownership of the system and, after much deliberation, agreed to convert it to electricity. It also added another eight columns to provide lighting for Burley Lane and Woodlands Lane. In 1938, the new system - involving glass reflectors and 150-watt tungsten bulbs - was switched on to operate, annually, from dusk to 11 pm, from 1st September to 30th April. But, in September the following year, World War 2 broke out and the lights were not switched on.

In September, 1944 (eight months before the end of the War in Europe), the Parish Council was given permission to introduce reduced lighting, using small power bulbs.

A year later the 150-watt reflector-lights were reinstated, and, in September, 1955, the East Midlands Electricity Board installed five more lights along The Common to *Beech Avenue Cottages*, bringing the total number of lights in Quarndon to 28.

In 1972, Derbyshire County Council installed 32 new sodium-type lamps along Burley Lane to the old boundary of Quarndon Parish (level with No. 133, *Holmwood*).

When the Montpelier development was built in 1965, Derbyshire County Council wanted to install ten mercury-vapour lamps. This was considered by Montpelier residents - and by the Parish Council - to be excessive and not in keeping with the rest of the village, but the only concession the County Council would make was that they would be of the sodium, not the mercury-vapour design.

Today most of Quarndon's street-light columns are of concrete and the bulbs themselves are of the sodium type, giving out a better light.

Modern electric street-light, Church Road

23. Cricket in Quarndon

Quarndon Cricket Club friendly: "Dads v. Lads". The last match of the 2007 Season

ALAST-OVER triumph at Lords; Border League and County League Champions; a Derbyshire Building Society Trophy hat trick; junior membership rising to 150. These are some of the achievements which fill the proud pages of the record books of Quarndon Cricket Club.

The Club dates back to 1884. The original Ground was opposite *Mulberry House* (the former Post Office) on The Common. In the early 1920s (because the farmer needed the land) it moved to the present Ground, further up The Common, where it commands spectacular views over Park Nook and Kedleston Park. According to Frank Stone, a past Captain of the Club: "The original Clubhouse was a converted hen-house until 1926 when a wooden building was erected, with separate dressing-rooms provided for home and visitors' teams and a central room for refreshments." He adds: "The rent to Lord Scarsdale was originally a bottle of brandy a year. Later it was increased to six bottles." (At the time of publication, the Club has a 25-year lease from the Kedleston Estate for two fields on commercial terms.)

To enhance the playing potential, an escarpment was created in the 1930s - thanks to the generous help of the late Arthur Richardson (see later in this Chapter) - to extend the level field of play to the west of the hallowed 'playing square'. During World War 2 this was converted into a tennis court to maintain it and prevent it from reverting into a meadow again.

The present Clubhouse was built in 1971. The walls are lined with pictures of star players - particularly those who featured in the golden years of the 1980s and 1990s.

Photo: Derby Evening Telegraph

The Clubhouse & Scoreboard in 1978

Whitbread Village Cricket Champions, Lords, 28th August, 1983

Back row, left to right: Frank Butcher, David Hibberd, Andy Acton, Martin Tunaley, Craig Richardson, Mick Coulthread, Nick Morris (scorer). *Front row, left to right*: Ian Farmer, Stuart Underwood (Vice-Captain), Bob Crossley (Captain), John Morris, Steve Hollis (wicket-keeper). (Ralph Taylor not in picture.)

Ian Farmer cutting the ball to the boundary, with Dave Hibberd, Man of the Match, at the non-striking end.

Quarndon joined the Border League in 1964 and won the Championship in 1980. But their crowning glory came on Sunday, 28th August, 1983, when Bob Crossley led the Quarndon team to face Troon in the (40-over) Whitbread Village Cricket Trophy Final at Lords.

Quarndon, on its first visit to Lords, was considered to be the underdog - Troon having won the Trophy in 1972, 1973 and 1976. But Crossley won the toss and put Troon in to bat. They scored 155 for 6 wickets (Quarndon's Ralph Taylor: 3 for 31; Frank Butcher: 2 for 21; John Morris: 1 for 34, with catches by Stuart Underwood and Steve Hollis, wicket keeper). In a nail-biting finish, Quarndon won the match, scoring 157 for 2 wickets in 39.2 overs.

The final ball was bowled shortly after half past six. The then Vicar of Quarndon, the late Arthur Milroy, who'd been listening to the commentary on BBC Radio Derby, admitted later that he'd never been so reluctant to cross the road to take 6.30 Evensong!

What he missed in Graham Richards's commentary was:

Photo: BBC Radio Derby

Graham Richards

"From the nursery end, Hibberd hoicks it, and it goes over the fielders, and that could be it - the ball, running away to the boundary, crosses the line and Quarndon have won with four balls to spare.

With this shot, Hibberd, the hero of the hour, takes his score on to 53, with his excellent partner, Farmer, on 38. Underwood scored 36 and Morris 14.

The rest of the side did not bat. Quarndon win, with 4 balls to spare, by 8 wickets, in a game that threatened to go to the last ball, but, in the end, didn't need to do so."

Hibberd, "hero of the hour", was named Man of the Match, and, to commemorate the victory, a weathervane - paid for by public subscription - was presented to the Club. It was designed to combine the Old Father Time weathervane at Lords with the Whitbread Trophy.

Left: **Back in Quarndon, Bob Crossley (Captain) parades the Trophy in front of Club members.**
Right: **The Weathervane.**

Three years later, Quarndon were Jackson Cup finalists in a match against Alvaston & Bolton at the County Ground.

Jackson Cup Finalists. *Back row, left to right*: **Chris Sanders, Chris Storr (Vice-Captain), Martin Tunaley, Mike Fletcher, Andy Acton, Bob Davis, Mick Thomas.**
Front row, l-r: **Dave Hibberd, Stuart Underwood, John Morris (Captain), Steve Hollis (wicket-keeper), Mel Godfrey.**

Left: 1st Division County League Champions, 1993. *Right:* **Silver Link Trophy winners, 1994.**
The Captain was Steve Hollis in both competitions.

In the early 1990s, in its desire to move forward to a higher standard of cricket, the Club recruited its first overseas professional - thereby no longer being eligible to compete in national **village** championships. After that, while continuing to play in County League 1st Division matches, the Club was able to compete in national **club** championship games. Quarndon were three times winners of the Derbyshire Building Society Silver Link Trophy and were champions of the Derbyshire County League in 1993.

Junior cricket training

Under the guidance of Steve Hollis (at the time of publication the Club's Cricket Chairman), the Club has a thriving youth section, with over 150 registered junior members, a number of whom are now progressing into the senior sides. Teams participate in the local leagues at Under 17, Under 15, Under 13 and Under 11 age-groups - a number of young players having gone on to represent the County. David Ball, the Club's Honorary Chairman for a number of years, writes: "Our emphasis is very much towards youth. More and more youngsters from the Quarndon area practise with us and more and more parents feel associated with the Club."

New scoreboard

Today the senior section of the Club boasts a First, Second, Third and Fourth XI and is a founder member of the Derbyshire Premier League - comprising the top twelve teams in Derbyshire. David Ball writes: "In the new cricketing pyramid, Premier League status is only granted to a limited number of leagues throughout the country. This makes us one of the top 260 competitive cricket teams in England and Wales. We are now also competing in the National Cup, which saw us reach the regional semi-finals in our first attempt in 2002 - losing to Harrogate, having beaten teams from Sheffield and Worksop on the way."

In September, 2004, a new practice net facility was formally opened by the then England opening bowler, Steve Harmison.

An electronic Scoreboard, which can be operated from the Clubhouse, was installed in 2006. (See *above left*).

Chris Storr, the Hon. Treasurer, adds: "So that cricket can continue to be played by future generations in the local community, the Club has recently embarked on an ambitious development plan. Majority funded by *Sport England,* this has included the acquisition of a second (adjacent) ground and a new outfield mower and roller. The square for this new ground was laid in the summer of 2007."

During the winter of 2005/6, the existing Clubhouse was refurbished and officially opened by Sir Viv Richards (the only West Indies Captain never to have lost a Test series). At the time of writing plans have been drawn up to extend the Clubhouse to provide changing accommodation for the second ground.

Quarndon's other connection with cricketing glory came with the late **Arthur Richardson** of *The Old Vicarage*, Quarndon, and, later, of *Quarndon Hall*. He was sales manager of W & J Richardson of the Eagle Leather Works, Derby - a company which, amongst other numerous products, tanned leather for cricket balls!

In 1936 he captained Derbyshire to the County Championship - the only time they've won the competition.

Since then, his son, William, and grandson, Alastair, have also played for Derbyshire.

(Sources for this Chapter: *Derbyshire County Cricket League 75th Anniversary Booklet; Whitbread Village Cricket 1984 Handbook*; Quarndon Cricket Club.)

The Village Hall
Above: The Institute or Parish Hall - fenced & gated. (Date taken unknown.)
Below: The Village Hall (formerly Church Hall) today,

24. The Village Hall

ALSO known originally as "The Parish Hall", "The Institute", and, until recently, "The Church Hall", the Village Hall was built by the Curzon family - assisted with funds raised by village efforts - on the site of a house belonging to Joseph Allcock (see Chapter 15: *Methodists in Quarndon*). It was opened by the Rev'd Alfred, 4th Baron Scarsdale (see pages 96 & 131), on 9th May, 1914, and, as our picture shows, was originally fenced and gated.

In April of that year a "Preliminary Announcement: Quarndon Parish Hall" stated that "Lord Scarsdale" had "completed the erection of this handsome and commodious Building" and that it would be "available for Concerts, Lectures, Amateur Theatricals, Classes and all Educational Movements at very moderate charges." (6 shillings, with an additional 1s 6d if fire or lighting were required. Parochial meetings free, except for lighting & heating). The announcement went on: "It is Lord Scarsdale's wish and intention that the Building shall be used as required by all the Inhabitants of the Village, and it is hoped that all will join in making it a real social centre and in bringing new interests into the Parish."

But, in 1919, a parishioner wrote to Lord Scarsdale (the former Viceroy of India, Foreign Secretary and son of the above) objecting to a plan to have "dancing and cards in the Parish Room on Saturday nights". Consequently, on 29th January, 1920, the Hall Secretary wrote to an applicant: "I am quite ready to give permission for the use of the Parish Hall for a Social. Lord Scarsdale, however, does not now wish any Dancing to take place in the Hall and it is, of course, on this condition that permission is given."

Certainly up to 1924 the Hall couldn't be put to secular use during Lent. In that year the Vicar, the Rev'd James Robinson, was outraged that the Women's Institute had organised a concert in the Hall on Ash Wednesday at the same time as a service was being held in Church!

In the "Great Sale" of 10th March, 1931 (see Chapter 28), the Hall was sold to the Diocese of Derby for £680.

Dated chimney-stack

155

Photo: Derby Evening Telegraph

This picture of a party in the Hall is thought to have been taken in the winter of 1940. (Note the snow on the corporal's greatcoat.) The then Vicar, the Rev'd Emmerson Richardson, is seated *4th from left* on *the second row*.

According to Frank Stone: "For a number of years, following the Second World War, there were regular dances to the band of Peter Ann (drummer) of *Quarndon House*. On New Year's Eve and Easter Monday there were fund-raising events for the Cricket Club and a Midsummer Dance was held in aid of the RNLI."

In 1965 the Hall was extended with an augmented stage, largely through the generosity of the late Hadden Richardson (See Chapter 18: *Other interesting houses*). In 1994 the Car Park was extended by the Parish Council to accommodate a total of 25 cars. The new land was the gift of William and Charles Richardson and Susan Perkins, in memory of their parents, Arthur Richardson (See Chapter 23: *Cricket in Quarndon*) and his wife, Gina.

The Hall is currently used by a number of local groups including: Lesley's Wednesday Workout, Quarndon Pre-School (aged 2-5), the Autumn Leaves (for the over-60s), Brownies, Quarndon Ladies' Club, the FACTS Club (Sunday School), SPY Club (10 to 14-year-olds), the Ecclesbourne Barn Dance Club, the Duffield Flower Group, the Historic Gardens Society, the Quarndon Amateur Dramatic Society, Quarndon Parish Council and the Quarndon Women's Institute, whose Wall Hanging illustrating current village activities is mounted to the right of the stage. (See Chapter 32: *Major celebrations & commemorations*.) It is also available for private functions.

The Re-opening Ceremony

The new Kitchen

The new Staircase

In the summer of 2004, as a result of funds being raised through the *Q'Spire* and subsequent appeals, the Hall was closed for six weeks while work was carried out to extend and refurbish the Hall, provide greater storage and better kitchen and WC facilities and install an internal staircase.

The total cost was £93,300.

Our picture shows the Re-opening Ceremony by the Mayor of Amber Valley, Councillor Glyn Hartshorne, on 24th September, 2004. Also pictured (*l-r*) are John Cunningham, the then Chairman of the Village Hall Committee; the Mayoress, Mrs Sheila Hartshorne; the Rev'd William Bates, Priest-in-Charge, St Paul's, Quarndon, and Councillor David Knight, Chairman of Quarndon Parish Council.

As a result of other fund-raising events, various improvements have been made to the Hall, including the purchase of new curtains, a new PA system, more tables and chairs and the replacement of all crockery and cutlery.

Quarndon Amateur Dramatic Society productions, 1946-1978

The Importance of Being Earnest, 1946

The Rivals, 1947

This was a Woman, 1957

Trap for a Lonely Man, 1970

Cock-a-doodle-do, 1977

The Full Treatment, 1978

25. Amateur dramatics & musical activity

AMATEUR dramatics have been a lively activity in Quarndon since the opening of the Parish Hall in 1914. A selection of post-World War 2 productions are illustrated on the opposite page and throughout this Chapter. But two black-&-white photographs shown here bear witness to some ambitious between-the-Wars spectaculars!

Rumplestiltskin, 1928

Pearl, the Fishermaid, 1929

The Hound of the Baskervilles, 1986   *Play On!*, 1994

Rehearsals were originally held in the large lounge of *Arranmore*, Coach Drive.

Ellen Hampshire, writing in 1931, lamented the passing of such earlier village entertainment as:

> "...the Wakes (when feasting and merriment ruled the parish for about a week), the 'Gaysers', the Morris dancers - with their concertinas and dulcimer, who were always sure of a warm welcome in every home at Christmas time, and without whom the gaieties of that Season would not have seemed complete - and the Brass Band, the members of which (who were all working men) would don their uniforms of navy blue with gold trimmings and enliven the village on Saturday afternoons and all holiday times with really good music. Alas! all these old customs have gone!"

But to trace the history of amateur musical and dramatic activity in the second half of the 20th century, the Editor is indebted to Thelma Ashton of Littleover for sending me a booklet called *The First Twenty-five Years*. The authorship is not disclosed, but Mrs Ashton writes that her father, F R Allison, a former parish councillor, was one of the three founders of the Quarndon Musical & Dramatic Society. The others (according to Frank Stone) were Arthur Handy and George Slack. As the booklet explains, two years into World War 2, "many of the young and middle-aged men were away in the Services and a number of womenfolk too were engaged on war service". Many who remained at home were Air Raid Wardens or First Aid workers, who were 'on call' most evenings. "The considerably curtailed bus service ceased altogether in the early evening and few people relished walking into town and back in the 'black-out'." The writer goes on: "It must not however be imagined that these conditions were as intolerable as they sound, for they actually created a spirit of comradeship which, alas, is seldom experienced in peace-time and the whole village was welded into a community."

In the Autumn of 1941, two men met at a post-box in the village - one posting a letter, the other walking his dog - and they hit on the idea of forming a musical society. They decided to enlist the help of Frederick Lockyear, a local retired schoolmaster, well-known at the time "for the promotion of large-scale Christmas concerts given by Derby school children". He agreed and a public meeting was held on 24th October that year. "There was an attendance of fifteen, which was considered very satisfactory. A Choir was set up and a Christmas Concert was held in the 'Parish' (now Village) Hall, which raised £13 14 6d for the Quarndon Services Comforts League."

On 2nd January, 1942, a General Meeting was held to inaugurate The Quarndon Musical & Dramatic Society, but "after considerable discussion it was felt that with so many men on war service there could be no dramatic activities until after the cessation of hostilities".

The Choir appears to have flourished and, later in the year, several concerts and an illustrated lecture on Beethoven's sonatas were organised. By the beginning of 1943 an Orchestral Section of the Society had been formed. (On hearing that a 'cellist was needed, one villager immediately bought an instrument and commenced taking lessons. In a comparatively short time she was able to take part!)

While the Choir tended to perform locally, the Orchestra went further afield, giving concerts in Derby and district and providing incidental music for an Ashbourne dramatic society. "But, after a successful season, some members left the district for business reasons, some became associated with larger orchestras in Derby and its numbers gradually dwindled until it eventually ceased to function."

Throughout the War period it had been Frederick Lockyear's dream to put on a Victory Concert. This was scheduled for 1st November, 1945, but, a few days before, he collapsed and died. However, the Concert went ahead as a combined tribute to him and a celebration of victory.

In September, 1946, it was possible for the Society to resume activities as a Dramatic Society. Meanwhile, for many years, an annual New Year Party had been held in the Hall, featuring sketches written and performed by villagers.

Man Alive, 2002

Changing Places, **November, 2003**

Little Photographer, **November, 2006**

The late Ursula Eddowes, who spent her childhood at Park Nook and later became Parish Council Chairman and a founder of Quarndon Youth Club, recalled:

"During the War, when my late husband, Dennis, and I were living in Derby, we put on several concerts for the troops. When we moved to Quarndon we organised similar concerts, with Dennis as producer and writer of the sketches and lyrics and composer of the music. We had enormous fun rehearsing and, by the reception we received, the audience also enjoyed them.

The first one we gave in Quarndon was in the 1950s in the Church Hall, which then was very basic. The stage was much smaller than now and the central heating was coal-fired. One evening something went seriously wrong with the boiler. Soon the Hall was filled with smoke - which caused some confusion, as you can imagine! - but the aged caretaker was called in and soon got it under control.

We put on two concerts for the Red Cross in the 1960s, but with no mishaps! By then the Hall had been much improved, the stage enlarged and the heating modernised - as indeed it has been again at the time of writing."

Tony Glover, who retired in 2006 as Chairman of the Quarndon Amateur Dramatic Society (QUADS), writes:

"With more than 120 productions staged since the end of World War 2, the tradition has been to produce two plays a year - one in April or May, the other in November. There's always a mix of drama, thriller and comedy played to critical acclaim from an audience of 330 per production, drawn from Quarndon and surrounding areas.

In 1991 and 2001 we celebrated the Society's 50th and 60th anniversaries in style, with formal dinners and celebratory productions. The Golden Jubilee saw a production of *The Importance of Being Earnest*, with a substantially new cast. This, we felt, testified to the popularity of QUADS, which continually seems able to renew itself, despite the apparent decline of amateur dramatics as a popular pastime. At the time of writing the Society has a membership of 32 - and could do with more (particularly youthful) members.

In the past couple of years we've put on a Village Cabaret - thus (as is borne out by the above) reviving an old tradition. Friends of QUADS was launched in 2006 and the Society is very grateful for the support of its patrons. We hope it will still be in existence in 2041 to celebrate its Centenary!"

A murder is announced, **May, 2003**

Outside Edge, **November, 2007**

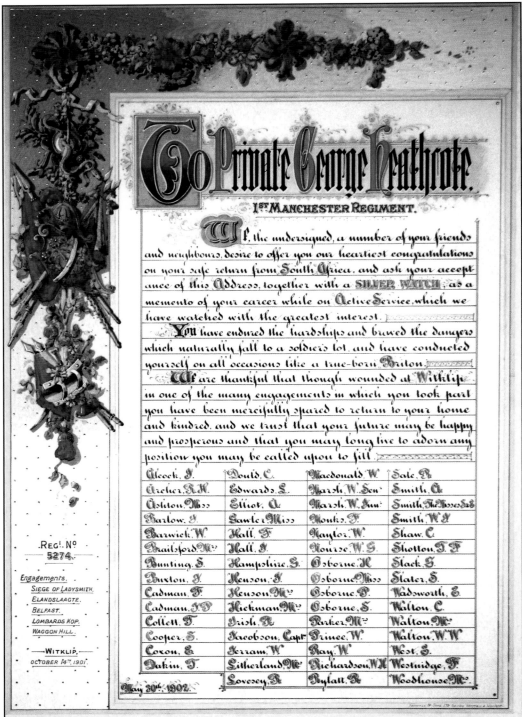

Courtesy: Michael Heathcote. Photo: Don Hall.

Boer War: Illuminated Address

26. Quarndon in Wartime

I: The Home Front & "foreign field"

WHETHER as participants in the fighting, or on the Home Front, or in celebrating and commemorating an end to hostilities, Quarndon was certainly touched by the four major wars between the mid-nineteenth and mid-twentieth centuries. In the two World Wars alone, the Somme, the Gallipoli Landings, North Africa, North West Europe, allied operations over Germany and the Burma Campaign all feature prominently in Quarndon's Roll of Honour.

On 29th April, 1856, a Peace Treaty was signed at the conclusion of the **Crimean War**. The then Vicar of Quarndon, the Rev'd William Henry Barber, presided at the "Peace Rejoicings" and dinners and teas were provided for every villager.

According to Ellen Hampshire: "In 1899, when the **Boer War** broke out, some volunteers were found in Quarndon - about 17 answering the call, all of whom returned safely." Among them - albeit having been wounded on 14th October, 1901, at Witklip - was 5274 Private George Heathcote of the 1st Manchester Regiment. He had taken part in the Siege of Ladysmith and the Elandslaagte, Belfast, Lombard's Kop and Waggon Hill engagements.

Courtesy: Michael Heathcote. Photos: Don Hall

On 30th May, 1902, he was presented with an *Illuminated Address* (see *opposite page*) - now the property of his grandson, Michael Heathcote - and signed by 59 villagers, including the Vicar, the Rev'd William Nourse, and the Headmaster, Robert Rylatt. It reads:

"We, the undersigned, a number of your friends and neighbours, desire to offer you our heartiest congratulations on your safe return from South Africa, and ask your acceptance of this Address, together with a SILVER WATCH" [see below, together with a tin of chocolates - given to George and all British soldiers serving in the War] "as a memento of your career while on Active Service, which we have watched with the greatest interest. You have endured the hardships and braved the dangers which naturally fall to a soldier's lot, and have conducted yourself on all occasions like a true-born Briton. We are thankful that, though wounded at Witklip in one of the many engagements in which you took part, you have been mercifully spared to return to your home and kindred. We trust that your future may be happy and prosperous and that you may long live to adorn any position you may be called upon to fill."

Anti-clockwise: **Private George Heathcote, silver watch, chocolate box.**

(George's mother died in the 'flu epidemic of 1918. George himself died in January, 1925, at the age of 47.)

Choir Stalls, St Paul's Church

Within three weeks of the outbreak of **World War 1**, a public meeting was held in Quarndon to support the *Prince of Wales's War Relief Fund* and to appoint a Parochial Distress Committee.

In 1914 - through subscriptions from a number of residents - gas street lighting was introduced in the village. (See Chapter 22.) But, a year later, John Argyle, Hon. Secretary & Treasurer of the Quarndon Street Lighting Committee, wrote to the Chief Constable of Derbyshire with concern that the lights might act as pathfinders for Zeppelins. "Of course," he wrote, "the lamps would be darkened on top, but would you kindly say if there is any order as to the number of lamps that may be lighted." The Chief Constable replied: "My own opinion is that lighting of the street lamps at Quarndon could not possibly do any harm or guide Zeppelins in any way. If they come over this part of the world their objective would probably be Sheffield. The line of the blast furnaces which runs up the Erewash Valley and then via Staveley and Eckington would be a much better guide for them than street lamps in any particular village." (Four months later, there were Zeppelin raids on Loughborough, Derby and Burton-on-Trent. Shortly after, street lighting was turned off for the duration of the War.)

In Chapter 6 it was explained that one of the original roles of the Lord Lieutenant of a County was to raise a local militia in times of emergency. In January, 1915, the Parish Council received a circular from the Lord Lieutenant of Derbyshire asking it to call a meeting "for the formation of a Corps of the Home Guard". At its May meeting that year a request was received from the Recruiting Officer at Normanton Barracks asking for the names of men in the village between the ages of 17 and 39. "It was unanimously agreed that the list be prepared at once, and this was, accordingly, compiled by the members." As Ellen Hampshire recalled: "In the Great War of 1914-1918, a member of almost every house in the parish (and in some cases two or three) was serving."

Those killed in the War, or who died after the War as a result of their wounds, are listed at the end of this chapter. The Choir Stalls in St Paul's Church (see *top of page*) were built "as a thank offering for the safe return of those of the village who served in the Great War, 1914-1918". The Choir Panelling and Vestry Screen were added "as a thank offering for the safe return of the men and women of this village who served in the World War, 1939-1945".

Peace Celebration Commemorative Mug, 1919

Front: Peace, Victory with Honour, Freedom, Justice

Reverse: Souvenir of the Great European War

War declared: Aug 4th, 1914

Armistice signed: Nov 11th, 1918

Peace signed: June 28th, 1919

PEACE CELEBRATION, 1919

Of those who survived World War I, George Beeson, Headmaster of the Curzon School, "suffered from the effects of being gassed in the War, and sometimes his temper got the better of him" (See Chapter 14) and Reg Moorcroft, the village cobbler, never recovered from shell shock. His brother, Harold (see *below*), who worked for Ley's Malleable Casting Company in Derby, won the Military Medal.

On 19th July, 1919, after the signing of the Treaty of Versailles, Peace Celebrations took place in the grounds of *The Grange*, Quarndon, with "track and field events and separate teas for children, ladies and men". In the evening there was dancing in the gardens of *Quarndon Hill*, followed by fireworks, from 10.45 to 11.30, in a nearby field.

On 11th October, the same year, a Dinner for 45 Ex-Servicemen was held in the then Parish Hall, when inscribed silver watches were presented to Corporal Charles Heathcote and Private Harold Moorcroft. The bill for dinner for 53 guests, 9 gallons of ale, 4 dozen bottles of Bass, 4 dozen bottles of mineral water, plus cigars and cigarettes totalled £26 18s 10d.

Unveiling the Memorial Cross

The Cross today

On 17th March, 1919, the Parish Council agreed that the War should be commemorated "in the form of a Monument or Cross on which the names of residents who have fallen should be inscribed".

The Grade II-listed **Cross** - based on the one on Iona - stands by the West Wall of the Churchyard. It was unveiled on 20th March, 1921, by **Lt-Col. C Herbert-Stepney** of Derby (see picture *above left*, to *left* of Cross) who, in World War I, had raised the 16th Battalion (Chatsworth Rifles) Sherwood Foresters. He lost his left arm at Ypres in 1917, was four times Mentioned in Despatches and won the DSO and Bar. He was supported by **Major-General Sir Reginald Hoskins** (same picture, *back right*) of Park Nook, who had won the DSO in the Boer War and had been Commander-in-Chief, East Africa, in World War I. It was dedicated by the Vicar, **the Rev'd Thomas Southey** (*right* of Cross). Following **World War 2**, the names of those servicemen killed in the conflict were added to the Cross.

The first major reference in the Parish Council minutes to **World War 2** appears in February, 1939 (seven months before the outbreak), when a circular from Belper Rural District Council asked for "help in finding homes for children from large towns during war time". It was agreed "to approach the various women's organisations in the parish, but at the same time to express the view that the major part of the village was unsuitable owing to its close proximity to the Borough of Derby". In April, 1940, after the Council had been allocated a possible 30 evacuees, it expressed the view that Quarndon should be considered a "neutral zone".

Villagers who were children in the War remember the searchlight battery at Quarndon Turn, the barrage balloons and the silver foil dropped by Allied aircraft to confuse the enemy.

Frank Stone recalls:

"The night World War 2 broke out there was an air raid warning. The village fire brigade (who used the engine at *Quarndon House*) all reported to their leader, Tom Handley - an Irishman - of *The Black Cottage*. But, in the rush, Tom had forgotten to put his false teeth in, so none of the crew could understand his instructions! Meanwhile, it was my job to cycle through the village blowing a whistle. But, before I could get out of the house, I was finding it difficult to put my clothes back on in the dark, to which my father remarked: 'By the time you've got yourself dressed, lad, bloody war'll be over!'"

There are complaints reported in the Parish Council Minutes (30.9.40) that children "are being sent home from school during an air raid warning" and that "adequate shelters should be provided for them while they are at school", and (30.3.42) that "stirrup-pumps, sand buckets, rakes, etc, are not yet provided at the school".

St Paul's Church Grade II-listed railings

When domestic wrought iron work was being confiscated for munitions manufacture, a resolution was passed unanimously "to support the Vicar's application for the retention of the iron railings which protect the Churchyard on the grounds that they form the sole fence and that their removal would establish a danger to pedestrians and expose the Churchyard to invasion by cattle." They were spared.

At *Quarndon Hill*, James Richardson's mother bred and exhibited Havana rabbits. James writes:

"There were twenty hutches - complete with 'toilet facilities'. The rabbits had lovely brown coats and my sister and I used to walk to Park Nook picking dandelion leaves for them to eat. Little did we know that the rabbit that regularly graced our dinner table was from one of those we had been feeding, or that their skins were being cured at our family tannery to make the warm mittens and hats that we wore in the winter!"

During the War much farmland had been neglected. Between 1944 and 1947 James remembers around 30 prisoners of war being brought in daily by bus from a camp at Sudbury to clear blocked ditches and install land drains. During the hard winter of 1947 they also cleared the snow from Park Nook and the lane to Windley. (The story of a prisoner of war from Clay Cross Camp who stayed on after the War is recounted at the end of this chapter.)

With food in short supply during and immediately after the War, James's sister, Judith, recalls that "swill" (potato peelings, cabbage leaves and all edible left-over food) would be collected from "houses with large families" to feed to pigs.

According to Frank Stone - who himself helped install the lighting in the famous tunnel at the Stalag Luft III ("Great Escape") Prisoner of War Camp - two survivors of World War 2 deserve special mention.

"Arnold Topliff, of The Common, having been taken prisoner by the Japanese, saved a fellow prisoner from drowning after the ship taking them to Japan was torpedoed. After repatriation he was awarded the British Empire Medal.

George Kelsey, who spent his childhood at *Bottom Farm* (see Chapter 8) was a navigator of Mosquito fighters. In April, 1944, he was awarded an immediate Distinguished Flying Cross for his part in a daylight battle when four of his squadron took on 14 Junkers 88 fighters. Later that year he stayed with a damaged aircraft and manually assisted the pilot to land safely in England."

The wartime minutes of Quarndon Women's Institute refer to a Billeting Committee, a Fruit Preservation Scheme, a Stalingrad Hospital Appeal and an *Aid To Holland* Fund.

Members were urged to save waste paper - particularly silver paper. By the middle of 1941 the supply of biscuits was "practically exhausted"; "tea only" would be served and, because of rationing, members should bring their own sugar. However, a Meals Service for Rural Workers and a Snack Meals Service were considered unnecessary in Quarndon.

Members were also asked to show hospitality to men and women serving with US forces and to US nursing staff - it even being intimated that "extra petrol would be available" to those who did so!

There are repeated appeals to help with an initiative to *Knit For The Forces* and for *Overseas Relief* - in fact there were problems in keeping up with the quota of wool being supplied. There were also appeals for furs, skins and fur-lined garments to be sent to Russia.

Wartime fund-raising campaigns

(The Editor wishes to thank Ann Ousley for undertaking the following research.)

Quarndon - along with 20 other parishes - joined the **Belper & District Savings Campaign**. This was part of a national initiative to encourage those at home to save money for the war effort through Savings Bonds, War Bonds, Defence Bonds and Savings Certificates and to pay deposits into Post Office Savings Banks. A hand-written ledger gives details of Quarndon residents' individual deposits - a painstaking task!

Warship Week (14th - 21st March, 1942)

Locally, this was for Belper & District to adopt *HMS Brocklesby* - a 'Hunt' class destroyer, which later took part in raids on St Nazaire and Dieppe, the invasion of Sicily and the Salerno landings. It became a training ship after the War. The Campaign was launched on screen at Belper's Ritz Cinema.

Quarndon target:	£3,000	Total raised: £10,544

Wings for Victory Week (9th - 17th April, 1943)

Quarndon target:	£3,000	Total raised: £7,628

Salute the Soldier Week (8th - 15th July, 1944)

Quarndon target:	£5,000	Total raised: £12,816

Thanksgiving Week (27th October - 3rd November, 1945)

Quarndon target:	£5,000	Total raised: £6,439

Overall Campaign target and total sum raised

Quarndon target:	£16,000	Total raised: £37,428

(£37,428 equates to £1.1m in 2008!)

There was also a nationwide **Dig for Victory Campaign.**

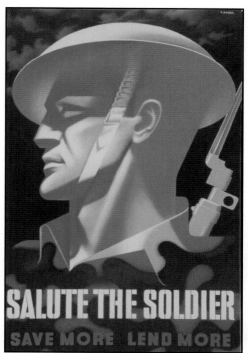

Edward Osmond. Imperial War Museum

Abram Games. Imperial War Museum

Crown Copyright. Supplied by Royal Naval Museum

Imperial War Museum

World War 2 posters

Photo: Don Hall

QUARNDON ROLL OF HONOUR

1914-1918

Boissier, William Arthur C.
Bull, Harry
Crossley, Erskine Alick
Dorell, Frederick
Dunstan, Eric
Fowke, William
Harness, Tom

Heathcote, Joseph
Hood, Reginald Smith
Moorcroft, Harry
Pearce, William Frederick
Revitt, Horace
Ride, Ernest
Scott, Alfred William

Winson, George

1939-1945

Broadhead, Eric
Brown, David
Burton, Charles
Holmes, Ewart

Irwin, John
Jaffrey, Walter
Knighton, Francis Sale
Stone, Walter Edward

Greater love hath no man than this, that a man lay down his life for his friends.

Roll of Honour

A Roll of Honour - bearing the inscription, "Greater love hath no man than this, that a man lay down his life for his friends"- lists the names of those men from Quarndon who lost their lives in the two World Wars. It hangs in the North Aisle of St Paul's Church Nave, with an accompanying Book (see *below*). The names are given on the following page.

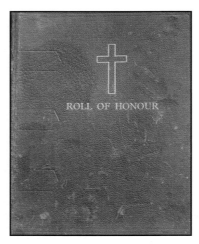

World War I

Lt William Arthur Boissier (27) Royal Marine Artillery. Accidentally drowned off Belgium, 27.7.17

Sgt Harry Bull 10th Battalion, Sherwood Foresters. 12.10.17

Capt Erskine Alick Crossley (Church Warden. The brass Altar Cross was given in his memory.) Died of wounds, 3.4.20

*Pte Frederick Dorrell (22) 4th Bedfordshire Infantry. 27.9.16

Pte Eric William Dunstan (25) 2nd/5th Sherwood Foresters. 9.9.18

William Fowke (41) Gassed in France, died 28.8.19

*Tom Harness (30) 4th Australian Infantry. 20.5.15

Pte Joseph Heathcote (32) 3rd North Staffordshires. Died from fever, 12.2.17

*Pte Reginald Smith Hood (31) (Member, Church Choir.) 9th Sherwood Foresters. Killed on landing at Dardenelles, 9.8.15

Harry Moorcroft (Taught at Quarndon School; member, Church Choir.) Post Office Rifles. Killed at Levee Wood on the Somme, 1916

William Frederick Pearce (23) 2nd Leinster Regiment. Killed in France, 12.4.17

Horace George Revitt (31) 5th Sherwood Foresters. 1.7.16

Ernest George Ride (Member, Church Choir.) 2/8 London Regiment (Post Office Rifles.) Killed at Bullecourt, 14.6.17

Alfred William Scott (37) (Member, Church Choir.) Died of wounds, 11.3.20. (His medal hangs over the Roll of Honour)

Pte George Winson (24) 3rd South Staffordshires. 10.4.17

* denotes name not recorded on War Memorial in Churchyard

World War 2

Gunner Eric Broadhead (21) RAF. Killed in operations over Germany, 23/24.5.42

Pte David Brown Killed on active service

Flight Sgt Charles Burton (29) 149 Sqdn, RAF. Killed in operations over Germany, 23/24.8.43

Pte Ewart Holmes (31) Royal Scots Fusiliers. Killed on active service in Burma, 16.5.44

Flight Sgt John Irwin (37) 12 Sqdn, RAFVR. Killed in operations over Germany, 9/10.7.43

Pte Walter Jaffray (28) 2nd Royal Warwickshires. Killed North West Europe, 20.7.44

Flying Officer Francis Sale Knighton (21) 500 Sqdn, RAFVR (Coastal Command). Killed off North African coast, 7.3.44

Pte Walter Edward Stone (23) (Frank Stone's brother) 4th Battalion, Royal Berkshires. Died in a bombing raid on the south of England, 30.9.40

From the other side

Widow of a German prisoner of war tells her story

MARIA MAIER, of *Beech Avenue Cottages,* **talks to JAMES RICHARDSON**

German prisoners of war, 1946. (Jack *far right*.)

Jack & Maria on their Wedding Day

"In March, 1945, my future husband, Johann (known later as Jack) - a signals operator in the German Army - received a dispatch from Adolf Hitler, ordering the officer in charge to fight to the last man. The officer, knowing that the situation was hopeless, tore up the dispatch, told Jack that he had 'never received it' and ordered his Company to drive into Belgium and surrender. This they did and were taken prisoner and shipped to England to a prisoner of war camp at Clay Cross.

Jack told me that the SS had always maintained that, if captured by the British, German soldiers would be tortured and killed. But, on arrival at Clay Cross, their hair was deloused and they were given a shower, clean clothes, food, a warm hut and bedding.

During the day - supplied with buckets, spades, pickaxes, bread and cheese and billycans for tea - they were taken by bus to local farms to help with hedging, harvesting, potato picking and land drainage. During the bitter winter of 1947 they helped clear the snow.

Though they often outnumbered their British guards by 10 to 1, it was all very relaxed (it was such a relief to be out of the war and safe!) and the farmers were very kind. By contrast, the economic state of post-war Germany was so desperate that several ex-prisoners of war - including Jack - stayed on to work on the farms.

In 1950 - along with 50 other German girls - I came to Derby as an *au pair* (in my case, initially at *Vicarwood*). The ex-PoWs soon found us and Jack and I married in 1951 at Derby Register Office. He worked as a farmhand and then as a boilerman at International Combustion. After retiring in 1985 he did gardening jobs around Quarndon. Then, at the age of 76, he became ill and died two years later in 1999.

Jack and I had seven children, who all went to the Curzon School. I now have seventeen grandchildren and one great-grandchild."

27. The Rolls-Royce connection

1: Sir Henry Royce

*(The Editor wishes to acknowledge the help and advice provided for this chapter by **MIKE EVANS**, Chairman Emeritus of the Rolls-Royce Heritage Trust.)*

Rolls-Royce Heritage Trust

Frederick Henry Royce, 1907

ON 9th July, 1908, Rolls-Royce's Nightingale Road factory was officially opened in Derby by John, later 2nd Baron Montagu of Beaulieu (an MP and pioneering motoring journalist). Around this time, the chassis line and the Company's registered office moved from Manchester to Derby. The previous winter had seen employees walking, cycling or travelling by horse and cart over the Pennines to their new premises and new homes!

On 26th June, 1907, **Frederick Henry Royce** - Engineer-in-Chief and a director of Rolls-Royce Ltd - had written from the Company's Manchester office to Henry Brailsford, estate agent, "of Park Nook, Quarndon", asking to look at "a house to let called *The Grange*", on the west side of Church Road. (In 1884 Royce had founded the Manchester company of F H Royce & Co, electrical & mechanical engineers. This became F H Royce & Co Ltd in 1894 and was re-launched on the Stock Exchange as Royce Ltd in 1899.)

A month later, Royce wrote again to say he'd seen the *The Grange*, but that it didn't suit him. He did, however, design *Holmwood* on Burley Lane - the land being bought on 21st November, 1910.

Under Royce's direction, such 'state-of-the-art' amenities as cavity walls, garages and a generating house were installed. (Maurice Oakley, who was born at *Burley Grange Farm*, recalls that, when his mother delivered produce to *Holmwood*, Royce would greet her with "Hello, my wench!" and give her a sixpence.) But he only appears to have lived there for a few months - probably in the summer of 1911 - until illness resulted in his leaving Derby.

Holmwood, 133 Burley Lane. (Extended since this photograph was taken)

While *Holmwood* was being built, Royce rented *The Knoll* (since re-named *Quarndon House*) on The Common. Our picture shows him outside *The Knoll* (perhaps in the late spring of 1911) with his 40/50 hp Silver Ghost-type car: *Chassis 1200*. (It was the first Rolls-Royce to be set aside specifically for experimental purposes and was sold in 1915 - the new owner having it fitted with an all-weather cover.)

Royce was a workaholic and it is said that what he had achieved over the period 1906-8 would have "finished off any normal mortal".

Claude Johnson, Rolls-Royce's Commercial Managing Director, expressed the view at the time that Royce had a tendency to supervise every aspect of the business to meticulous standards and that he should be distanced from the factory so that the whole of his efforts might be devoted to his genius as an engineer. He also hoped that it would ease the burden that Royce carried and thereby prolong his life and the contribution he could make to the Company.

Royce with *Chassis 1200* outside *The Knoll*

Courtesy: Ian W Rimmer

The same car
This was described as "Mr Royce's red upholstered grey body". Royce is at the wheel with his wife, Minnie, in the front passenger seat. Violet Punt (see *opposite page*) - from whose photograph album the *top right* picture came - is on the near side of the rear seat.

In the meantime, on 12th July, 1910, the Hon. Charles Stewart Rolls, Royce's co-founder of the Company, became the first British pioneer aviator to be killed in an air crash. The following year Royce was taken seriously ill and underwent an operation. He recuperated at Overstrand, Norfolk, and, during the winter of 1911, was taken on a grand tour of the Mediterranean by Johnson. (His wife, Minnie, disliked overseas travel.)

During their tour, Johnson introduced Royce to Le Canadel, near St Tropez, with the hope that he would fall in love with it - which he did - almost immediately building a villa there. On his return to England, Royce and Minnie took a house in Crowborough, Sussex.

There is said to have been a memorandum between Johnson and Royce's brother-in-law, Ernest Claremont (who was Chairman of the company and had worked with Royce since 1884) stating that "we must find a nurse for" (Royce), "for he is not one to seek outside the house that which he can find within it".

Sure enough, after another illness, Royce spent the rest of his life with his nurse, Ethel Aubin - either in the south of England, or, during the winters, at Canadel. Minnie initially remained at Crowborough with her niece, Violet Punt, whom the Royces had adopted as their daughter.

Royce was created a baronet in 1930 and died in 1933. *Holmwood* was bought by Albert G Elliott (pictured *right* in the early 1950s, outside the house with his Rolls-Royce *Silver Wraith*). He had been Royce's principal design assistant from 1914 - at Le Canadel and in the south of England. "Wherever Royce was," it is said, "so too was Elliott." But in 1932 (much to Royce's chagrin) Elliott moved back to Derby, where, ultimately, he was appointed the Company's Chief Engineer. In 1951 he became Joint Managing Director with Ernest (later Lord) Hives and, in 1954, Executive Vice-Chairman to Hives. He retired in 1955.

Albert G Elliott at *Holmwood*

Two distinguishing features of *Holmwood* are its tall garages (*left*) to accommodate early Royce models and (*right*) the Generator House (now the summer house of *Holmwood Cottage*, 135 Burley Lane).

Courtesy: Ellen Cholerton

Courtesy: Jonathan & Sheila Balmer

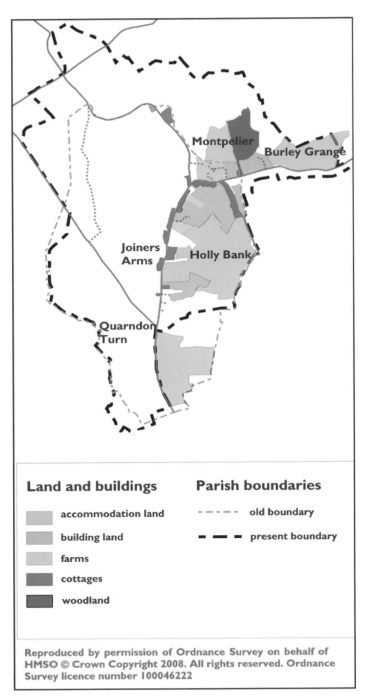

Land and buildings

accommodation land

building land

farms

cottages

woodland

Parish boundaries

– · – · – old boundary

— — present boundary

Montpelier

Burley Grange

Joiners Arms

Holly Bank

Quarndon Turn

Reproduced by permission of Ordnance Survey on behalf of HMSO © Crown Copyright 2008. All rights reserved. Ordnance Survey licence number 100046222

Quarndon properties affected by The "Great Sale" of 1931.
Map by Matthew Pitt

28. The "Great Sale" of 1931

The Scarsdale Collection

**Marquis Curzon
1ˢᵗ Viscount Scarsdale***

ON 10th March, 1931, in Richardson & Linnell's St James's Sale Rooms, Derby, 3,600 acres of land, "comprising the outlying portions of the Kedleston Estate", were put up for auction. This was held to pay off the death duties incurred by the estate of Lord Curzon of Kedleston, first Viscount Scarsdale (1859-1925), former Viceroy of India and Foreign Secretary.

The 145 lots included "two country inns, two sand quarries, plantations, sixty-three cottages and fifty-two farms and small holdings in the parishes of Turnditch, Hulland Ward, Ravensdale Park, Mugginton, Weston Underwood, Hazelwood, Windley, Duffield and Quarndon". To this the sale catalogue adds: "Also valuable accommodation land at Quarndon and Duffield, ripe for immediate development."

According to Ivan Cope: "It was all very traumatic. People fell out with each other in the Sale Room and became enemies overnight. Those with families were threatening to buy houses and evict those without families."

The map on the *opposite page* shows the areas for sale in (what, since 1984, is now) Quarndon.

By Instructions from The Right Honourable Viscount Scarsdale

DERBYSHIRE

Particulars, Plans and Conditions of Sale
OF A PORTION OF THE

Kedleston Hall Estate

In 145 Lots comprising
TWO COUNTRY INNS
TWO SAND QUARRIES   PLANTATIONS
SIXTY-THREE COTTAGES
FIFTY-TWO FARMS AND SMALL HOLDINGS

Part of sale catalogue cover

The catalogue mentions "good deposits of sand and gravel in Bunkers Hill, which could be worked with but little difficulty". However, Bunkers Hill, *Botany Farm, Church Road Post Office, Vine Cottage* and *Holly Bank Farm* are all marked "WITHDRAWN". It's also interesting to note that the prior sale of properties outnumbered sales at the auction.

Burley Grange Farm (35 acres, farmhouse and outbuildings, now demolished) fetched £1,500; *Burley Wood*: £200; *Montpelier Farm* (22 acres, farmhouse and outbuildings, now demolished): £650; the Parish (now Village) Hall (sold prior to auction): £680; *The Quandary* (100 Church Road) - together with outbuilding and paddock - £525 and the *Joiners' Arms*, plus outbuildings, garden and land (sold prior to auction): £2,300. *Sunny Hill* and *Sunnyside* (163 & 165 Burley Lane) and the *Black Cottage* were also sold prior to auction. The lots also included over 140 acres of "accommodation land" and "building land" in the Quarndon area.

Nine of the lots in Quarndon carried the rider: "Formerly copyhold of the Manor of Little Chester (see Chapter 6) and is subject to the Lord of the Manor's interests in the minerals.

(*George Nathaniel, Lord Curzon, in the robes of Chancellor of Oxford University. Portrait by Sir Hubert von Herkomer, Kedleston Hall. The Scarsdale Collection was acquired with the help of the National Heritage Memorial Fund and transferred to the National Trust in 1987. ©NTPL/John Hammond)*

Welcome to Quarndon!

Top left: Roland Darvell; *top right*: Rose Doman (mother of Edna & John); *centre* (in glasses): Bob Allen; *bottom left*: John Doman; *bottom right*: Joan Darvell; *2nd & 4th right*: Brian & Ivor Darvell

Source unknown

29. Quarndon in Wartime

2: The evacuees tell their stories

READERS who remember World War 2, or have heard from parents and grandparents about school children being evacuated from London, will have mental pictures of frightened, bewildered youngsters in their thousands - labelled and carrying gas-masks - being herded on to trains bound for the unknown. Conflicting accounts, however, emanate from some of the former pupils of a school in Essex. On 2nd June, 1940, pupils from Chalkwell School, Leigh-on-Sea, Southend, were evacuated to Quarndon, where, between them, they recall various close encounters with German bombs.

As **Edna Blake-Dawson** (née Doman) - who was 13 when she was evacuated with her brother, **John** - told the *Southend Echo* in later life: "Talk about 'The Darling Buds of May', we were evacuated to a farm! It was wonderful!"

John wrote the following for *Quarndon: Then & Now*:

"Hoards of children waited on Southend Station to board the trains. It was terribly exciting - and fascinating to see our teachers far more worried than we were! We hadn't the faintest idea where we were going, but travelled towards Fenchurch Street Station, London. The train slowed and pondered through industrial areas of London that I hadn't seen before, then sped up north and I thought 'Yippee, Scotland, here we come!' and made it known through the entire rowdy carriage!

Later, we pulled up at a station and waited a long time, but, eventually, an old charabanc-type bus, with smoke pouring out of the back, took us to Quarndon - to alight at the Church Hall, on the top of the hill.

A number of nice, cheerful people welcomed us inside, and then we were picked out and taken to our billets. Edna and I were last, but she insisted that we stay together, so a Mrs Kirkland, who'd expected to take two boys, condescended to have us.

Edna & John with their parents

It was late, we were very hungry, and off we went down the road to *Fir Tree Farm*" [thought to have been somewhere between 33 and 41 Church Road]. "There we were introduced to Mrs Kirkland's son, George; Tom, the Irish farm labourer; Charlotte, the old housekeeper, and Rover, the dog (who wasn't much good at cow-herding, but I managed to teach him a trick or two of my own!) The weather was glorious and we had great fun exploring our new, exciting and expansive home."

In the meantime, added Edna, their mother, who'd been evacuated with them on the same train, but in another carriage, got 'mislaid'!:

"She'd alighted at a station where drinks were being provided, and, on her return, discovered that our part of the train had been shunted off! A week later, Mr Curtis, our headmaster from Leigh-on-Sea, located her in Weston Underwood and she joined us at *Fir Tree Farm*. Soon after, our father, a corporal in the Royal Engineers who'd returned from France, was posted to Castle Donington for three months and spent his leave - including Christmas - at the farm. After the traumas of France, he loved the tranquillity of an English village."

John continues:

"With an old T-type Ford made into a low-loader, Edna and I - on our own - chain-harrowed a whole field. Then came the harvest, with all the hard work in the fields - the cutting, the stooking, the carting, the stacking and then the threshing-machine: a great red box, towed and operated by a huge steam engine. I remember the dust, the noise and the sweat. But what an excitement!

I remember walking up the hill to school. Edna was taught in the school building itself by the headmaster, Mr Beeson (see Chapter 14: *Quarndon's schools*); I was taught in the Church Hall by Miss East from Southend, who, I recall, took an instant dislike to me and I to her! After school a friend and I would hurtle down the hill on his bike - with me on the crossbar.

The brook at the back of the farm was a great play area, as was the old churchyard across the road, with its ruined tower - a great venue for war games!

There was a shop nearby where we would buy sweets or a paper packet of five Woodbines or Park Drives. These we shared out and smoked in a den by the brook.

John & Edna Doman on a DIY see-saw. (Two bombs fell in the trees behind.)

John Doman, on a visit to Quarndon, pointing to where the two bombs fell among the trees.

I remember the air raids and the bombing. They were said to be targeting Rolls-Royce in Derby and the anti-aircraft and searchlight battery at Quarndon Turn. Many a night we spent down a very cold, dank cellar under the farmhouse. One night, after the 'All Clear', we went out into the farmyard thinking it was daylight. All along the skyline was bright yellow and crimson. It was Coventry - which burnt for three days and three nights! On another night there was this horrendous and continuous explosion. Bottles fell out of racks and plaster off walls. In the morning I ran out to find trees stripped of their bark or blown over, plus two huge craters - one in the field behind the farm, another in the brook. I gathered up a considerable amount of shrapnel and handed it out to my best friends at school."

(In April, 1941, a solicitor in Quarndon wrote to a colleague in Scarborough: "We had a couple of bombs at the bottom of the hill - somewhere at the back of *Old Croft*." [*Old Croft House*, 23 Church Road.] "There is a searchlight in the field at the road junction and it was evidently a shot intended for them. I believe only a few panes of glass were cracked.")

Not all the evacuees, however, enjoyed such a status of equality with their host families. With his sister, **Joan**, and twin brothers, **Brian** and **Ivor**, 10-year-old **Roland Darvell** arrived in Quarndon on the same evening as the Domans. For the first night they were split up - his sister to one house, his brothers to another and he to a farm. He recalls waking up on the first morning:

"The first thing I heard was all these farm noises: a cockerel, bird songs and a mixture of animal noises. I recall going into the yard and meeting two young women in Land Army uniform. I then learned that my two brothers had spent the night crying because they'd been separated from me. So we were all taken to a Mr & Mrs Ann, who lived in a large house near the Church." [*Quarndon House*, 46 The Common - see page 126.]

183

"Mr Ann was Managing Director of the Midland Drapery Store in Derby. Apart from Mrs Ann, the house was run by three ladies: a parlour maid, who always wore black dresses with a white apron and starched head dress, a cook and a general housekeeper. There was also a gardener, a stable man and other occasional jobbing men - all of mature age.

Although we slept in the principal bedrooms, we were not allowed to use the front stairs to the entrance hall. We had to leave and arrive via the servants' quarters, which we used for meals and social purposes. However, I occasionally had interesting chats with Mr Ann and, on a couple of occasions, Mrs Ann took me fly-fishing and I ate the fish we caught for supper.

I sang in the St Paul's Church Choir (a good preparation for my appearances in adult life with the Southend Operatic Society) and helped pump the organ during choir practices.

I recall buying a bicycle from a local boy for five shillings. But the transaction didn't survive the night because his mother demanded the return of the bicycle. It was made known that the sharp practices of London and the South East didn't go down well with her and I was not the right sort of boy to mix with her son!

In the Anns' garage was a fire engine (see *below*) - about quarter size, I think - just like the ones you could buy as toys, but big enough for adults to drive and stand on.

I particularly remember the night the bombs fell. We were taken to a safe area of the house and in the morning were told that a bomb had landed on Bunkers Hill. We went to see the crater, but none of us was particularly impressed or frightened. Maybe small children are more sanguine than adults!"

The Quarndon Fire Engine
- surrounded by members of the Quarndon Auxiliary Fire Service.
The late Peter Ann, in whose parents' garage the Engine was kept, is seated *far right*.

Photo: *Derby Evening Telegraph*

Watching the Match

Two other arrivals on 2nd June, 1940, were 7-year-old **Bob Allen** (in glasses in the *middle* of the picture on page 180) and his brother, **Peter**, who was only 4 - the youngest of all the evacuees.

Bob has vivid memories of two events: a snowball fight between the local children and the evacuees and a local cricket match where the evacuees were the spectators. They were photographed by the *Derby Evening Telegraph*, and, as he told a *Telegraph* reporter on a visit to Quarndon 60 years later: "I remember Mr Ann bought dozens of copies of the paper and gave it to the evacuees so they could cut out the picture and send it to their parents."

James Richardson and Bob & Peter Allen playing in the garden at *Quarndon Hill*.

Bob, James & Peter outside the cottage at *Quarndon Hill*, where the Allen brothers had stayed.

185

Audrey Bowers (*left*) and her sister, Muriel, in Mr & Mrs Fisher's garden at *Darrock*, Kedleston Road (Muriel's billet).

The following year, **Audrey Bowers** & her sister, **Muriel**, were aged 11 and 13, respectively, when they came to Quarndon. They were first billeted at *Park Nook*, where they "lived in the servants' quarters" (now separated as *The Georgian House*) "with the maid and the cook, collected milk in enamelled cans from *Park Nook Farm* during the week and had tea with the family - including their son, 'Mr John' - on Sundays". They then moved to separate houses on the Kedleston Road - each with a couple who had no children.

Muriel recalls: "During air raids, we had a superb underground shelter in the house. An unexploded bomb fell in the field on the opposite side of the Kedleston Road, so we were very lucky." Audrey says: "I sang in the Church Choir and, from time to time, we were called out of school to sing at funerals - a new experience! I often went home down the hill on the boys' bikes, sitting on the handlebars. Once we missed the corner and I shot over the hedge into a field!"

Both speak very affectionately of Mr Beeson, the headmaster (see Chapter 14) - "a good teacher and a kind, understanding man, who let us play Shinty" [a version of Hockey] "in the adjoining field, kept ducks in the playground, and, in the summer, would get the village boys to carry our big heavy desks outside in the sunshine".

When Muriel left to go to another school, her hosts gave her a bound copy of *Black Beauty*, inscribed: "With best wishes. In remembrance of a three months' stay in Quarndon during the war year, 1941." Audrey, who went away to high school in Cheshire from Quarndon, writes: "Mr Beeson presented me with *The Concise Oxford Dictionary*, which I still treasure. Considering we were so far from home, I can look back on Quarndon with much warmth and affection."

According to John Doman, when his school returned home in July, 1942, they did so "with vivid, loving and thankful memories of Quarndon".

30. The Rolls-Royce Connection

2: The Cromwell Tank

Source: **W A Robotham: Silver Ghosts & Silver Dawn** *(Constable, 1970) and* **MIKE EVANS**

OUR picture (probably taken in 1942) shows a Cromwell tank undergoing trials on the field on the southern corner of Burley Lane and the A6. (You can identify the tree - still in existence - on the hill on the north side of Burley Lane.) The trials field is also the site of the Burley Hill Pottery (see **Chapter 4**). Apparently post-War archaeologists remarked how small the pottery fragments were!

By 1937 Ernest Hives had been General Manager of Rolls-Royce for a year and saw the need to divide the Company's operation into two Divisions: Aero Engine and Chassis. Then, when War broke out, all engineering staff moved to Belper, with W A Robotham, who lived at *Park Leys* on Cumberhills Road, being put in charge of the Chassis Division. But all car chassis production was stopped for the duration of the War, so Robotham settled on applying the skills of his team to the improvement of tanks, which, says Mike Evans, "they did to good effect in developing the Cromwell".

Burley Hill trials

This was carried out at the Clan Foundry on the A6 in Belper. Mike Evans writes:

"Robotham's team looked at how to install an alternative to the American World War I Liberty engine. They decided to adopt the world-famous (27-litre) Merlin engine (because it was bigger, more modern, more powerful and in full production for the RAF) and modify it into the Meteor engine. But, initially, the Meteor's power broke gearboxes, transmission and other parts, as well as creating cooling problems, so the team had to set about developing the cooling system, transmission and suspension.

(The tank hulls, incidentally, came from the Birmingham Railway Carriage & Wagon Works.)

Then, at the end of 1942, Rolls-Royce took over the work Rover had been engaged in on the (Frank) Whittle jet engine, while Rover took responsibility for the Meteor tank engine."

By D-Day (6th June, 1944), the Cromwell had become capable of well over 40 mph in service (other tanks managed about a quarter of that speed) and many did up to 5,000 miles without full servicing. Later, the Government launched the Centurion tank with the same engine. It sold worldwide.

Photo: Les Parkin

Brian Clough, 1979, when Nottingham Forest won the European and League Cups

One Saturday evening in 1979, Brian was at a Chinese restaurant in Derby, proudly displaying the two magnificent cups his Nottingham Forest team had won. Back in Burley Lane, Quarndon, the photographer Les Parkin received a telephone call from Brian inviting him to come over and take some pictures. When he heard that the Parkins were entertaining Quarndon friends, he invited them along too - including Jim Keane (pictured *left*) of Burley Drive, Quarndon.

31. The Brian Clough years

By PAT PARKIN

IN 1982, when Brian Clough - the best known name in British football at the time - chose to make his home in Quarndon, it brought an air of great excitement and pride to the village - particularly among sports lovers and children.

Since 1967, when he became manager of Derby County Football Club with his long-term deputy, Peter Taylor, he had become known all around the sporting world for his successful management techniques, his lively personality and his unique ability to put pride back into football. He loved the game he had devoted his life to and wanted others to share in his success.

He had played football for England, and when forced to retire because of a serious injury, he decided to try management. When still only 30 years old he became the youngest manager in the Football League, going on to win the First Division Championship with two clubs - Derby County and Nottingham Forest - taking the latter to the top of Europe by winning the European Cup twice in successive years.

Everyone admired his skills of man management, his ability to motivate and his unrivalled charisma. Not surprisingly, his name was soon linked with the England manager's job. It was something he wanted more than anything else in football. But, though the FA interviewed him on one occasion, in their wisdom they chose Ron Greenwood. It was a decision which forever after made him known as "the best England manager that England never had" - a tagline that stuck with him until the day he died. It was even mentioned by his devoted widow, Barbara, at his Memorial Service in Pride Park, following his death in 2004.

By that time, the Clough family had moved on from Quarndon, but Cloughie, as many knew him, was never forgotten, and many villagers who knew him as a neighbour and friend went along to Pride Park to pay their respects.

During his lifetime he had never been afraid to speak his mind, whoever it might upset. He was brilliant at conjuring up good quotes for the Press and media and, inevitably, that attracted a media circus.

Photos: Les Parkin

1970s Clough
Clearing the snow at the Baseball Ground

1970s Clough
Signing autographs at a local store

Photo: *Daily Express*

Brian walking up The Common
Snowdrop Cottage (before it was painted white) can be seen in the distance.

Large contingents of reporters would chase around the village seeking his views. It must have annoyed the Clough family and it certainly irritated some residents. But, faced with pushy sports reporters or gossip-mongering newsmen, Quarndon folk became adept at pointing out the wrong house, claiming the family were away or feigning they knew nothing - all to put them off the scent!

But he loved life at *The Elms* on The Common, with its outlook over the Cricket Club at the front, its beautiful garden and view across the Derwent valley to Duffield Bank at the back. He was also a familiar sight in the village with his golden retriever, Del.

Says Barbara: "I shall always look back on Quarndon as being an important part of our lives. Our children liked it too, and people were very kind and supportive - especially during the time that Brian was ill." She particularly remembers Frank Juffs - "a wonderful artist, whose daughter was also a gifted artist and valued friend".

She also speaks warmly of the Geesons at *Snowdrop Cottage* on The Common. "I will never forget Doris Geeson," she says. "She hailed from Buxton originally and knew Vera Brittain, author of *Testament of Youth* and mother of Shirley Williams. Doris, like her, had interesting opinions on politics and women's place in society. She was a strict vegetarian and a very forward-thinking woman, who remained a source of interesting conversation and wonderful humour until she died in her 90s. Her husband, Alfred, grew their vegetables and was very proud of his apple tree, which he'd grown from seed. His home-made wine was often the cause of a certain hesitance while walking back to my home further down The Common. (Our lovely neighbour, Margaret Fearn, would testify to this!)"

Another of the Cloughs' close friends in the village was the late Gordon Warrington, who, with his wife, Eileen, kept the *Quarndon Stores* in the 1980s. (See also Chapter 12: *Shops, trades & industries*.) Says Barbara: "Gordon was an especially nice man - an excellent cricketer and interested in all sports. He and Brian had many chats putting the world of cricket and football to rights, while Brian sampled a delicious cheese."

Eileen says: "We enjoyed our time in Quarndon and Brian was a very regular customer. One thing I suspect quite a few villagers may not know is that, every week without fail, he would call in and hand over £20 - or sometimes £30 - to pay for food parcels for the residents of the Old People's Bungalows. He was a very generous man like that and did a great deal for others without any fuss. I remember the day after Gordon's funeral I was in the back of the shop and he called in to have a word to see that I was all right."

Eileen continued: "He had an opinion on everything, and though some people thought he could be a bit rude, it was just a case that he didn't suffer fools gladly. Many, I think, will remember him as a kind-hearted man who loved being with other people."

Though he was best known for his role in the world of football, Brian Clough was also someone deeply interested in politics. He was a great supporter of the Labour Party and was often invited to speak at public meetings. In fact there was a time when many people believed he might even pursue a political career himself.

Alas, the loss of the Post Office on The Common and, finally, the closure of the *Stores & Post Office* on Church Road, contributed to the Cloughs' departure from Quarndon. Of all the well-known people who have lived in the village, few could match the character, wit and personality of the man who gave himself the nickname 'Old Big 'Ead'. This, he assured everyone, was the reason the Queen gave him the honour of an OBE!

Photo: Les Parkin

March, 1995

Brian is invited back to the Baseball Ground as guest of honour - seated here next to the then Rams' owner, Lionel Pickering. He received a tumultuous welcome.

Roy McFarland recalls...

Roy McFarland (born 1948) was signed as a central defender for Derby County by Brian Clough and Peter Taylor in August, 1967. The side won promotion to the First Division and followed this success with two league titles - Roy winning 28 caps for England. In 1981 he became player manager at Bradford City, bringing the club promotion in the 1981/2 season. In 1982, he returned to Derby as assistant manager, becoming manager in 1993. Since then his career has included manager of Bolton Wanderers, Cambridge United, Torquay United and Chesterfield Town.

Linda, Roy & Beth McFarland at No. 14 Woodlands Lane in the late 1970s.

"Linda and I moved to Quarndon on our return from honeymoon in 1973. Our daughter, Beth, was born here, and, for us, it's the perfect place to live and has been our home ever since. Sometimes people tell me I'm 'living in Clough's village', but I always point out that I was here before him!

Brian Clough was fantastic to me and helped my career a great deal. He and Peter Taylor had the belief that football was simple and uncomplicated. Brian did things differently from other managers and was very thoughtful. When the team was away from home for a while, he would send flowers to wives with a note saying he was sorry to keep their husbands away for so long. He had old-fashioned values and really cared about people.

He had a marvellous career, but, sadly, didn't live as long as he should have done. He's been greatly missed in the football world."

32. Major celebrations & commemorations

NO village history would be complete without coverage of its celebrations and commemorations of major events. But, apart from the *Illustrated Address* presented to Private George Heathcote on his safe return from the Boer War and the memorials in St Paul's Church and Churchyard (see Chapter 26: *Quarndon in Wartime: The Home Front & "foreign field"*), Quarndon appears to have no pictorial record of how it marked the end of World War 1 or 2, or of the four coronations which took place in the twentieth century. However, records of other celebrations have survived.

(a) Royal Jubilees

© National Portrait Gallery, London

Queen Victoria

According to the *Derbyshire Mercury* of June, 1897: "**Queen Victoria's Diamond Jubilee** was observed in Quarndon with as much enthusiasm as any place in the country. It was decided to place a **Striking Clock** in the tower of the Parish Church, in addition to entertaining the parishioners to dinner and a meat tea.... The Brass Band marched on to a large field at *The Grange*. The band played the National Anthem, etc, and dinner and tea were served in a large marquee to 150 men and 280 women and children. There were 20 sports events and Jubilee mugs were presented."

The Church clock

Frank Stone recalls: "**George V's Silver Jubilee** in **1935** was commemorated by the planting of **an Oak Tree** (see *right*) behind the bus shelter and telephone kiosk by the Church Hall. I took part in the planting.

When World War 2 broke out, in case of invasion, an explanatory plaque - along with all other name-plates - was removed from the tree.

In 1963, as Parish Clerk, I dug a hole to erect a concrete plinth on which to reinstate the plaque. But that was the day of the Great Train Robbery in Bedfordshire.

George V Silver Jubilee Oak

© National Portrait Gallery, London

King George V

The following day there was a knock at my door...

It was the Police, who asked me: 'Why were you digging a hole?'"

Queen Elizabeth II

HM The Queen

© National Portrait Gallery, London

IN AID OF
QUARNDON CORONATION CELEBRATIONS
—

An Olde Tyme Dance

will be held on
JANUARY 16 TH 1953
at the
CHURCH HALL, QUARNDON

ADMISSION 2/6   REFRESHMENTS

Coronation Dance ticket

TO COMMEMORATE
THE SILVER JUBILEE
QUEEN ELIZABETH II
1952 - 1977

Jubilee Seat plaque

Fund-raising in Quarndon to celebrate the **Coronation of Queen Elizabeth II** in **1953** amounted to just over £144 - an **Olde Tyme Dance** (& Raffle) raising £18 10s 5d.

To commemorate her **Silver Jubilee** in **1977**, a **Seat** (replaced for the **Golden Jubilee** in **2002**) was placed outside the Senior Citizens' Bungalows. To celebrate the event, two **Tea Parties** were organised - one for **Children**, one for **Pensioners** - in a marquee on the Cricket Ground.

Silver Jubilee Children's Tea Party in Cricket Club marquee

Silver Jubilee Pensioners' Party in Cricket Club marquee

Other events celebrating the Silver Jubilee included a **Children's Sports Day**, a **Barn Dance** and a **Bonfire & Barbecue** on Bunkers Hill.

Everything was financed through a **Village Grand Prize Draw**.

In **2002**, local celebrations of the **Queen's Golden Jubilee** were organised by the *Q'Spire* **Committee** (raising funds for the Church spire and Village Hall). They consisted of a **Street Party** on Montpelier, including an **All-age Tea**, a **Children's Face Painting Demonstration** and a **Conjuring Display**.

This was followed by a **Hog Roast, Dance & Firework Display** on the Cricket Ground.

Photo: Janet Turnbull

Golden Jubilee Street Party, Montpelier

Golden Jubilee Street Party Tea

Face-painting

The Rev'd William Bates, Priest-in-Charge, St Paul's, Quarndon, cutting the Golden Jubilee Cake.

Photos: Janet Turnbull

Conjuring Display

(b) Celebrating the Millennium

(i) Open Gardens; Flower & Art Festival

There was a **Village Open Gardens Weekend** and a **Combined Flower Festival & Local Art Exhibition** in the **Church.**

Photos: David Widdows

(ii) The Millennium 'Big Day'

The Millennium Act of Worship   *Pastel by Robert Hamilton*

On **Saturday, 22nd July, 2000**, the Cricket Ground was the venue for the **Millennium 'Big Day'**. The event began with a **Millennium Act of Worship**, conducted by the then Bishop of Derby, the Rt Rev'd Jonathan Bailey, the Rev'd William Bates, Priest-in-Charge, St Paul's, Quarndon, and the Bishop's wife, the Rev'd Susan Bailey, Associate Priest, Quarndon, accompanied by the Curzon Church of England School Choir (Choirmaster: Paul Hunter). This was followed by **Children's Races, Kwik Cricket, Putting, Slalom Golf, Croquet, Skittles, Boules** and a **Tug-of-War**, followed by **Tea** and an **Evening Barbecue & Dance**.

Tug-of-War

Children's Fun Fair

Photos: David Widdows

Kwik Cricket

Children's conjurer

Big Day prize-winners

Evening revellers

(iii) Millennium Variety Show

Photo: Derby Evening Telegraph

To raise funds for the Millennium festivities and commemorations, a **Variety Show** was put on in the **Village Hall,** then repeated by popular demand!

Our picture shows performers of the (almost) *Full Monty* - together with the 'Spice Girls'. *Back row, left to right:* Adrian Daley, Margaret Fearn ('Posh') - who replaced Mary O'Neill in the second performance - Gérard Varin & Tony Bennett (Master of Ceremonies). (Mike O'Neill, the fifth member, not shown). *Front row, l to r:* Jane Burgess ('Sporty'), Lesley Kirkland ('Scary'), Lesley Etwell ('Ginger'), Chris Short ('Baby') & Robert Kirkland.

Other Millennium events included **Line Dancing, Quiz Nights**, a **Horse Race Evening, Aerobics**, a **Golf Tournament** and an **Auction Supper**.

(c) Commemorating the Millennium
(i) Millennium Mug; Church Weathercock; WI Wall Chart

To **commemorate the Millennium**, the **Church Spire Weathercock** was re-gilded, a **Millennium Mug** was distributed to every villager under 18, and **Quarndon Women's Institute** produced a **Collage Wall Chart of Village Activities,** which is mounted in the Village Hall.

Photo: David Widdows

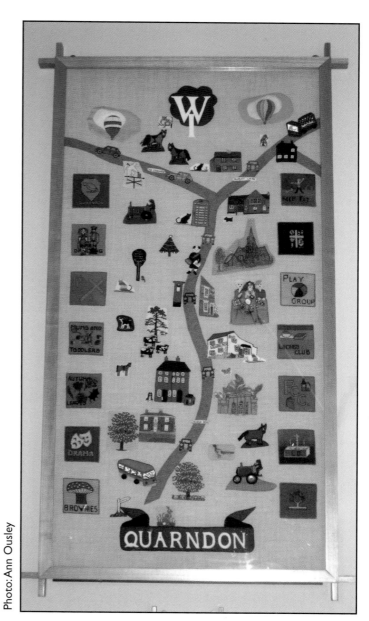

Photo: Ann Ousley

(ii) Topograph & Seat; Human Sun Clock; Time Capsule

Professor Jonathan Powers, the Hon. Richard Curzon & Lady Scarsdale at the Unveiling

Photo: David Widdows

On **29th September, 2001** (delayed by the previous year's foot-and-mouth epidemic), a **Millennium Topograph** was unveiled on Bunkers Hill - part of the Kedleston Estate - by Helene, Viscountess Scarsdale, and her son, the Hon. Richard Curzon. It was in memory of Francis, 3rd Viscount Scarsdale, who had died before the project was completed.

The Topograph was the brain-child of Professor Jonathan Powers, who lives at *The Quandary*, Quarndon (see Chapter 16). He said at the Unveiling: "When I first moved here, I was astonished by the view from Bunkers Hill - as far as the Crich Memorial, the Nottinghamshire Wolds and Charnwood Forest. But what were all those towers, chimneys and churches? And what was their history? I wanted to find a way of decoding the landscape."

The Topograph is a metre-diameter stainless steel "directional compass" standing on an 8-ton block of Derbyshire gritstone, 420 feet above sea level. It provides details of the bearings, distances, elevations and dates of nearly 50 places of special interest - either clearly visible from the Hill or hidden from view just over the horizon. 18 local sites - including Milford and Peckwash Mills, Breedon-on-the-Hill, Pride Park Stadium, East Midlands Airport control tower and Duffield, Breadsall and Spondon Churches - are accompanied by etched illustrations.

Photo: David Widdows

The Millennium Topograph

The total cost of the project - including the design and manufacture of the Topograph disc and the purchase and erection of the stone - was nearly £6,500. £1,000 of this was met through fund-raising events during Quarndon's Millennium celebrations, plus a £500 anonymous contribution towards the stone. The rest was provided through a grant of £4,000 from the Heritage Lottery *Awards for All* scheme and £1,000 from Quarndon Parish Council.

Photo: Jonathan Powers

Lowering the Topograph stone into position.

Quarndon Parish Council

This Topograph,
in memory of
Francis, 3rd Viscount Scarsdale,
was constructed and erected
with funds raised by
the villagers of Quarndon
and supported by the
Heritage Lottery
Awards for All Scheme.
It was unveiled by
Helene, Viscountess Scarsdale,
and the Hon. Richard Curzon
and dedicated by
the Rev'd William Bates,
Priest-in-Charge of Quarndon,
on 29th September, 2001

The Topograph plaque

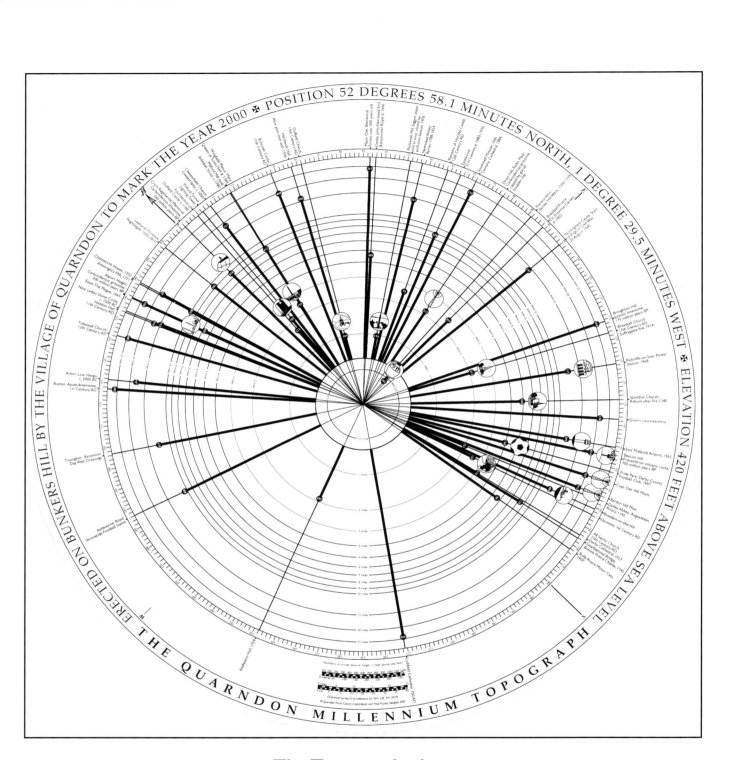

The Topograph plate

Manufactured by Smith of Derby, Ltd

Designer: Mike Fitchett

Photo: David Widdows

**Bryan Harris, Millennium Committee Chairman, unveiling the Millennium Seat
with Vicki Allison**

Also at the ceremony, a **Millennium Seat** was unveiled by Vicki Allison, who donated it to the village in memory of her husband, Dr Robert Allison of Quarndon, Consultant Anaesthetist to the Derby Hospitals.

In **2004**, a **Millennium Human Sun Clock** was laid in the grounds of the Senior Citizens' Bungalows.

Our pictures show *left:* Olivia, Charlie, Phillip & Claire Varin, and *right:* Esther & Isobel Lamb demonstrating the Sun Clock.

The Millennium Human Sun Clock

Finally, a **Millennium Time Capsule** lies somewhere under Quarndon's turf - not to be opened until the year 2,500. In the meantime, may it rest intact and be exhumed in glory!

(d) Quarndon wins *Best Kept Village* Competition

Quarndon was in the Medium-sized (500 - 1500 population) category of the Competition.

Top: Winners, 1977

Middle right: Winners, 1985

Bottom right: Winners, 1992

Photos: *Derby Evening Telegraph*

33. Quarndon through the seasons

Sunrise from Park Nook, November, 2007

Daffodil Time. *Top:* Woodlands Lane. *Bottom: Vine Cottage,* Church Road

Photo: David Widdows

Daffodil Time: Church Road

Daffodil Time: The Chalybeate (From the South)

Bluebells, Park Nook Wood

Quarndon in bloom. *Top*: No. 121 Church Road. *Bottom*: No. 22 Church Road

LONGFIELD HOUSE
No 22

Autumn: Coach Drive, October, 2003

Photo: Tony Glover

Photo: Tony Glover

Senior Citizens' Bungalows, October, 2003

213

The Common, October, 2003

Photo: Tony Glover

Top: Daytime moon. *Bottom:* Bath Plantation (No. 93 on *Field Map*, page 38)

Photos: David Widdows

Sunset through Bath Plantation. (Taken from Cannon Hill.)

Photo: David Widdows

Frosty Quarndon, December, 2006. The Common.

Frosty Quarndon, December, 2006. *Top:* **Woodlands Lane.** *Bottom:* **Spiders' webs, 99 Burley Lane**

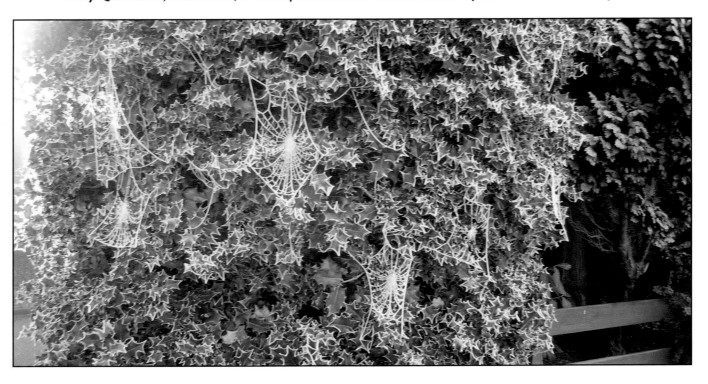

Photos: *Derby Evening Telegraph*

Quarndon in the snow. *Top: Park Nook Cottage* **and (what is now)** *Park Nook Grange,* **February, 1960.**
Bottom: **Church Road. (Date unknown.)**

Quarndon in the snow. *Top:* View from Inn Lane. *Bottom:* The Chalybeate.

Snow drifts, Inn Lane

Photos: David Widdows

Christmas in Quarndon. *Top*: **No.21 The Common.** *Bottom*: **The Village Christmas Tree, Church Road.**

Photos: Les Parkin

34. Quarndon: *A family walk*

By CLARE TURNER

(Questions & answers in *blue italics*)

Before you start

Remember the Green Cross Code:

- Think first ... **find the safest place to cross then stop**
- Stop ... **stand on the pavement near the kerb**
- Use your eyes and ears ... **look all around for traffic and listen**
- Wait until it's safe to cross ... **if traffic is coming, let it pass**
- Look and listen ... **when it is safe, walk straight across the road**
- Arrive Alive ... **keep looking and listening for traffic while you cross**

And please observe the Country Code:

- **Enjoy the countryside and respect its life and work**
- **Guard against all risk of fire**
- **Keep dogs under close control**
- **Keep to public paths across farmland**
- **Use gates and stiles to cross fences, hedges and walls**
- **Always close gates after you**
- **Leave livestock, crops and machinery alone**
- **Take all litter home**
- **Help to keep all water clean**
- **Protect wildlife, plants and trees**

Please note:

There are ramps up to the Old Churchyard.

Church Rd has a gradual incline.

From Montpelier to the Topograph is 450 m, approx. Plus 2 stiles & a sloping field.

As you walk through the village, look out for lions! How many can you spot?

Start your walk at the Old Chapel on Church Road, near Old Vicarage Lane.

(For more information see Chapter 2: *Quarndon's Chapel*)

- Be careful! Uneven ground.
- Yew and ivy - don't touch! These plants are poisonous.
- Don't walk on or between the graves.

**Quarndon's Chapel
19th century photograph
(From Church Road)**

The path today

- *What does the Chapel look like today?*

This is how the Chapel tower looked when the Nave was demolished. ▶

◀ Because it was so entwined with ivy, the tower was left standing.

- Now go to the middle of the front row of gravestones. Look for Thomas Barton's grave.
- *What was his job?*
- *Thomas Barton is called 'late'. What does this mean - 'not on time' or 'dead'?*
- *Thomas's wife, Eliza, was buried here too. Why do you think her surname is different?*
- *There is a carved anchor at the top of Thomas Barton's gravestone. Why do you think it's there?*
- *Look at Eliza Simpson's tomb under the yew tree by the entrance to the churchyard. What animal is carved at the top? Why was this animal chosen?*
- *Find the Richardson vault, built in 1871. How many bricks do you think it is lined with? How long do you think it took to build? How much do you think it cost?*

Anchor: Thomas Barton's gravestone

Eliza Simpson's tomb

The Richardson vault

- *Today, the Chapel is an ivy-covered ruin.*
- Quarndon had a place of worship from the 12th century. The old Quarndon Chapel had a tower with a turret and two bells. It was demolished in 1873-4.
- In 1821 the Churchyard was consecrated. This meant that people could be buried there. Thomas Barton's must have been one of the first graves.
- *He was master of the Free Grammar School.*
- In 1835 Quarndon's Free Grammar School was called a 'respectable boarding academy for young gentlemen'. It cost 21 guineas (£22.05) for a year's board and lessons. The school was at *Old Croft House*, 23 Church Road, across the road from the churchyard. 30 boys were taught there.
- *'Late' means 'dead'.*
- *After Thomas's death, she remarried. Her name changed to Sowter.*
- *Anchor stands for hope and being a loyal Christian.*
- *A lion is carved on Eliza Simpson's tombstone. It stands for courage, nobility and God's power. (The lion is known as 'the king of beasts'. A carved lion is said to guard against evil).*
- Following the death, in 1871, of William Richardson (of the leather tanning company), a family vault was built in the Churchyard.
- *The invoice from Charles Hampshire states that the work involved lining it with 2,700 bricks. It took just over 20 working days to complete and cost £11 10s 11d (£11.56p).*

**Walk up Church Road for about 400 metres. Stay on the pavement.
Just past *Holly Bank Farm*, look for the stone milk churn stand.**

(For more information see Chapter 8, *Farming in Quarndon*.)

Milk Churns

- *Who used to put out the churns there? What would happen to them?*
- *What animals would you have seen in the field near the churn stand?*
- *How is milk collected from farms today?*

- Until World War 2, there were 12 farms in and around Quarndon. Today, only *Botany Farm* (off the Common), *Park Nook Farm*, *Bath Farm* and *Champion Farm* (partly in Quarndon) are still working farms.
- *The dairy farmer would put out the churns, to be collected by the milkman.*
- *Farmers raised cattle, including Friesian and Jersey cows, for milking.*
- *Today, milk is generally collected from farms by tanker.*

Look across the road to *Vine Cottage*, Nos. 53-57 Church Road

- *Can you see a structure rather like a metal shed opposite the cottages? What do you think it is?*
- *Why do you think the cottages (originally one cottage - see p. 84) are built at right angles to Church Road?*
- *What do you think passed this way?*

**The transformer
today**

- *The structure is an electrical substation - one of several in Quarndon. These are used to transform high voltage electricity down for domestic use. (When electricity first reached Quarndon in 1912, the supply was transformed by a 'Bobby's Hat' transformer opposite* Vine Cottage).
- *The cottages are built at right angles to Church Road because Battelle's Lane - one of Quarndon's oldest roads - ran in front of them on its way to The Kedleston Hotel.*
- *A coach and horses used to pass this way, going from Derby to Manchester.*

**'Bobby's Hat'
transformer**

Walk up the hill for 30 metres to the Chalybeate Spring

(For more information, see Chapter 10: *The Chalybeate*.)

- Look carefully through the gate of the Spring.
- *What animal's head can you see used as a spout for the spring water?*
- *What famous writer visited Quarndon in 1727? How do you know this by looking at the Spring?*
- *What famous shipwreck story did he write?*
- *The water temperature was about 9° Centigrade. How would a bath have felt?*
- *If the Spring was still running, what do you think Quarndon might be like today?*

- You pronounce the word Chalybeate "Cal - lib - ee - at". The name means that the water has iron in it. It's a very old word that comes from *chalybs*, a word for 'hard iron' used by the ancient Romans.
- *People drank the water from the lion's head pourer.*
- The castle-like structure was probably built in 1760. It had an attendant's room, behind the door on the left, and a bath. In 1663 the water was said to be, amongst other things, 'good against vomitting, comforts ye stomach, cures ye ulcers of ye bladder'.
- *A plaque on the back wall states that Daniel Defoe visited the Spring in 1727. He had written the famous shipwreck story 'Robinson Crusoe' in 1719. (He said about Quarndon: 'We found...the waters good, and very physical, but wretched lodgings and entertainment.')*
- *A bath would have felt very cold! (The temperature of a warm bath is about 40°Centigrade.)*
- Children used to fill jars from the lion's head and sell the contents for sixpence.
- A series of earthquakes stopped the flow of water from the Spring. The first earthquake was in 1863. The flow of water finally stopped in 1956.
- *If this hadn't happened, Quarndon could have been a spa town like Bath!*

Walk a few metres up the hill to *The Joiners' Arms*

(For more information, see Chapter 9: *Quarndon's Pubs*)

- *How do you think the pub got its name?*
- *What animal is on the pub door?*
- *What differences can you see between the two photographs?*
- *How many pubs did Quarndon once have?*

- *The name dates from the 1760s when The Joiners' was frequented by craftsmen building nearby Kedleston Hall.*
- *There is a lion's head knocker on the front door.*
- *In the old photograph, The Joiners' is not painted; it doesn't have an extension and the entrance is on Church Road.*
- *Quarndon once had at least five pubs! They included The Pig & Whistle, The Tiger, The King's Head (now The Quandary on Church Road - see Chapter 16) and The William IV.*

> **At *The Joiners' Arms*, cross the road very carefully.** Remember the Green Cross Code!
> **Walk up the pavement until you are next to No. 101 Church Road.**
> **The building right by the pavement is the old Butcher's Shop.**

(For more information on shops in the village, see Chapter 12: *Shops, Trades and Industries*.)

- *The butcher sold meat very cheaply just before he closed the shop on Saturdays. Why do you think this was?*
- *There were marks on the east wall of 101 Church Road before it was rendered. What clues did they give about the old butcher's shop?*

101 Church Road, before and after the east wall was rendered.

- *In the days before refrigeration, the butcher had to sell off meat before closing time on Saturday, as it would not have kept fresh until Monday.*
- *On the 'before' photograph of 101 you can see (l to r) where the shop window, Post Office box and door used to be.*
- **Stop Thief!** There is a gruesome story about Quarndon's butcher. He used to collect his meat from Derby with his pony and trap. Several times somebody robbed him as he came back to the village in the dark. One night he caught the thief in action. He got out his cleaver, which is a heavy knife. The thief got away, but minus two fingers!

Walk up the hill towards the Curzon School

- When you get level with *Holly Bank*, No. 88, look across the road at the house. Can you see a stone trough at road level? This was a favourite drinking stop for horses pulling carts up Church Road.

- *How do you think the trough was kept full?*
- *What animal's head can you see on the black and white door of the house?*

- *The trough was filled by stream water via a pipe at the top.*
- *There is a lion's head knocker on the door.* (Another Lion!)

The Curzon School

(See Chapter 14: *Quarndon's Schools*.)

- Look at the plaque on the *Old School House* wall and in the School Crest.
  - *What can you see that is the same? What could be the reason?*
  - *What does the school's crest mean?*
  - *What do you think it was like for the children 100 years ago in the old school?*

- The Curzon School was founded by the Reverend Alfred, 4th Baron Scarsdale, in 1859. He built the *School House* in 1861.

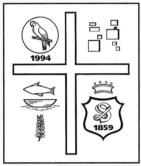

The School Crest

- *The 'S' on the wall and in the School Crest stands for 'Scarsdale'.*
- *Bottom left: The Ear of Corn refers to the "quern" (hand-operated corn-grinder) of 'Quarndon'. The Fish - like the Central Cross - denotes the School's link with Christianity.*
- *Top left: This "perched parrot" must originally have been intended to represent the Rising Popinjay in the Curzon crest. 1994 was the year the School became Grant Maintained (until 1997).*
- *Top right: These are the building blocks of education.*
- *Bottom right: This is the Scarsdale Coat of Arms - 1859 being the year the School was founded.*
- *The School had a big open fire in the Infants' Classroom, separate playgrounds for boys and girls, windows nearly 2 metres above the floor, outside toilets and no electricity!*

Walk up the hill to St. Paul's Church

(See Chapter 19: *St. Paul's Church*, and Chapter 26: *Quarndon in Wartime*.)

- *What trees can you see in the churchyard that you saw by the ruins of the Old Chapel? Why might they be there?*
- Look up at the church. *What carved heads can you see on the four corners at the base of the spire? What do they stand for?*
- Look at the clock on the spire. *How old do you think the clock is?*
- *Why do many churches have a clock?*
- *Where can you find five references to the First and/or Second World Wars inside and outside the Church?*
- *How many Quarndon servicemen lost their lives in the two World Wars?*

- *Yew trees have been traditionally associated with churchyards for centuries. They were sacred to the Druids and historically have been associated with rebirth - perhaps from the ability of their branches to root if they touch the ground.*
- The wood of this poisonous tree is renowned as the material used to make the English longbow, vital at the Battle of Agincourt in 1415.

- *At the four corners at the base of the spire are carved heads representing the four Evangelists (Gospel-writers). Starting from the South-West corner, clockwise, they are: the Man (Matthew), the Lion (Mark), the Ox (Luke) and the Eagle (John).*
- *St. Paul's clock was installed in 1897 to mark Queen Victoria's Diamond Jubilee.* **(In 2004 it was upgraded to global positioning accuracy.)**
- *Places where people gathered together, like churches, had a clock in the days before most people could afford their own watch.*
- *References to the two World Wars are: Inside (i) Memorial in North Aisle, with (ii) Roll of Honour Book; (iii) carved inscription in the North Choir Stalls; (iv) Brass Plate on wall behind the South Choir Stalls. Outside: (v) Memorial Cross in the Churchyard.*
- *23 Quarndon servicemen lost their lives in the two World Wars.*

Walk past St. Paul's Church to the Church Hall

(See Chapter 24, *The Village Hall*)

- Look at the chimney stack at the side of the Hall.
- *What does 'S 1913' stand for?*

- *'S 1913' stands for 'Built by Baron Scarsdale, 1913*
- Opened in 1914 and extended and refurbished in 1965 and 2004, the Village Hall is home to many village activities - from plays to playgroups.
- Look at the map on the wall. It's great for local information.

Walk to *Pinfold Cottage*, 226 Burley Lane and look across at the wall.

(See Chapter 6: *Village law, order and government*)

- *What was the wall in the picture part of in the past?*

- In medieval times there was more open land. Sometimes people's animals strayed and damaged other people's property.
- A man called a Pinder caught them and put them in a pen called a Pinfold. The owner had to pay a fine, usually about one penny, to get their animal back, and pay for any damage.
- *This wall was part of Quarndon's Pinfold.*

> **Walk along the pavement towards Woodlands Lane.**
> ***The Black Cottage* is on the corner on the right.**

(See Chapter 12, *Shops, trades and industries*)

- *Why was* The Black Cottage *popular with walkers?*
- *How much do you think a ginger beer or five caramels at* The Black Cottage *would have cost you in old money?*

- *There was a teashop in an iron shed next to* The Black Cottage *where people could buy refreshments, parkin (a kind of gingerbread) and sweets.*
- *A ginger beer or five caramels cost one penny.*

> **Walk approximately 100 metres up Montpelier from Burley Lane and turn right at the footpath sign. Turn right again when the path between the houses meets the main path. Follow the footpath, behind the houses, and cross a stile. Walk past Burley Wood on your left and cross another stile into a field. Walk up the slope to Bunkers Hill and the Millennium Topograph.**

(See Chapter 32, *Major celebrations and commemorations*)

The Topograph is a circular steel plate set in Derbyshire gritstone. It gives information about landmarks and events past and present.

Can you find:

- *How far you are above sea level?*
- *A Cathedral?*
- *Robin Hood's tree?*
- *Rammie's home?*

(Answers are on the Topograph plate.)

> **Retrace your steps back to Montpelier.**
> **Hope you've enjoyed your walk.**
> **Time for a ginger beer!**

Some Quarndon Lions
There are lions at:
- The Old Churchyard
- The Chalybeate Spring
- *The Joiners' Arms*
- *Holly Bank's* white door
- St. Paul's Church ▶

See if you can spot some others. Look up!

35: *Postscript*

By Quarndon Parish Council

QUARNDON enjoys a unique position as a village community, largely surrounded by Green Belt and situated between the city of Derby and the rural town of Belper - both offering opportunities for employment, shopping and leisure. It is very much a 'garden village' - in close proximity to Allestree Park and the (recently-designated) Derwent Valley Mills World Heritage Site - with access by numerous footpaths to spectacular Derbyshire countryside. The air is healthy and Quarndon's winding roads and lanes command magnificent views of Duffield Bank, Crich Stand, *Kedleston Hall* and the hills of Charnwood Forest.

While the Parish Council laments the loss of services provided by the Stores and the Post Office and the ministry of a full-time Vicar, it supports the aspirations and achievements of the Curzon School and the work of the Priest-in-Charge of St Paul's Church, Quarndon, in combining this responsibility with those of St Nicholas', Allestree. It congratulates the Cricket Club for its success in attracting children and young people to become playing members. It also supports the Village Hall and the organisers of *Quarndon Events*, in providing all-age entertainment and raising funds for extra village amenities.

Planning continues to represent a major part of the Council's interest and activity. We are acutely aware that some building projects and alterations have met with controversy, but we continue to make the strongest representations to the Borough Council, as the planning authority, to prevent unsympathetic developments. It is the Parish Council's aim to retain the pleasant rural nature and scale of the village street scene while maintaining harmony between the community as a whole and those submitting planning applications.

The Council is actively concerned about the speed and volume of traffic passing through the village. Speed restriction signs are clearly visible and appeals to the County Council to impose a weight restriction of 7.5 tons on all unauthorised vehicles travelling through Quarndon will continue until action is taken. It is also hoped that, with the prospect of steady rises in fuel costs, improvements in bus and rail links will reduce the local use of cars and commercial vehicles.

On aspects of law, order and crime, the Council appreciates the vigilance of the police community support officers assigned to the area and the efficient reporting systems set up by the local Neighbourhood Watch.

It is hoped that villagers derive maximum use and enjoyment from the Millennium Topograph and Seat on Bunkers Hill, the Jubilee Seat and Human Sun Clock on Church Road, the Children's Play Area by Barn Close and the many activities provided by local organisations.

At the time of publication, the Parish Council meets in the Lower Village Hall on the first Monday of the month (except in August), when public participation is welcomed. To find out more about the services provided by the Council and other village events, you're invited to visit the Council's website on **www.quarndon.parishcouncil.net** If you have any items of general interest which you think should be included on the site, please don't hesitate to send them by e-mail to **enquiries@quarndon.parishcouncil.net**

David Knight (Chairman), Ann Ousley (Vice-Chairman), John Cunningham, Richard Curzon, Bryan Harris, Paul Hodson, Matthew Pitt, James Richardson, David Widdows.   >>>

Quarndon Parish Council
Chairmen since its First Meeting, 13th December, 1894

1894-1897	W M Richardson
1897-1898	W J Smith
1898-1907	Henry Brailsford
1907-1910	Alfred Smith
1910-1917	Henry Brailsford
1917-1921	The Rev'd Thomas Southey
1921-1922	Thomas Shotton
1922-1923	Alfred Mee
1923-1925	The Rev'd James Robinson
1925-1926	F H Wright
1926-1938	James Coy
1938-1946	Thomas Hanley
1946-1963	W S Tunley
1963-1966	Mrs Margery Sulley
1966-1969	Cyril Weston
1969-1970	Kenneth Woodall
1970-1973	Colin Raybould
1973-1976	G W Richardson
1976-1979	Mrs Ursula Eddowes
1979-1983	Clive Richardson
1983-1987	David Widdows
1987-2004	Bryan Harris
2004-	David Knight

If you would like more copies of *Quarndon: Then & Now*, they are available at £5 each (plus post & packaging) via: then&now@quarndon.parishcouncil.net